FEB 2009

CULTURES OF THE WORLD®

ANDORRA

Byron D. Augustin

mc **Marshall Cavendish**
Benchmark
New York

PICTURE CREDITS
Cover: © The Photolibrary Wales/Alamy
Alfredo Maiquez/ Lonely Planet Images: 12, 43, 72 • Audrius Tomonis: 135 • Christian Kober/ Getty Images: 106 • Donald C. & Priscilla Alexander Eastman/ Lonely Planet Images: 94 • Francesc Muntada/Corbis: 49 • Francis Tan: 120, 130, 131 • GeoEdventure-Byron D. Augustin; GeoEdventure-Timothy R. Staskus: 6, 7, 8, 9, 10, 13, 14, 15, 34, 36, 39, 40, 44, 46, 52, 55, 56, 57, 58, 60, 63, 64, 67, 70, 75, 79, 81, 82, 83, 85, 86, 89, 95, 96, 97, 98, 100, 102, 103, 121, 129 • Jed Jacobsohn/Getty Images: 108 • Julian Finney/Getty Images: 110 • O. Alamany & E. Vicens/Corbis: 20 • photolibrary.com: 1, 3, 4, 5, 11, 16, 17, 18, 19, 23, 30, 31, 45, 48, 53, 54, 62, 74, 76, 78, 104, 123, 124, 126 • Reza/Getty Images: 112, 117 • Shannon Nace/ Lonely Planet Images: 50 • STEPHANE DE SAKUTIN/AFP/Getty Images: 26 • Vatican Pool/Getty Images: 35 • Warren Little/Getty Images: 109 • Wayne Walton/ Lonely Planet Images: 68

PRECEDING PAGE
A group of Andorrans skiing.

Publisher (U.S.): Michelle Bisson
Editors: Christine Florie, Stephanie Pee
Designer: Lynn Chin
Copyreader: Kristen Azzara
Cover picture researcher: Connie Gardner
Picture researcher: Thomas Khoo

Marshall Cavendish Benchmark
99 White Plains Road
Tarrytown, NY 10591
Web site: www.marshallcavendish.us

© Times Media Private Limited 1997
© Marshall Cavendish International (Asia) Private Limited 2009
All rights reserved. First edition 2009.
® "Cultures of the World" is a registered trademark of Times Publishing Limited.

Originated and designed by Times Media Private Limited
An imprint of Marshall Cavendish International (Asia) Private Limited
A member of Times Publishing Limited

All Internet sites were correct and accurate at the time of printing. All monetary figures in this publication are in U.S. dollars.

Library of Congress Cataloging-in-Publication Data
Augustin, Byron.
  Andorra / by Byron D. Augustin.
        p. cm. (Cultures of the world)
  Summary: "Provides comprehensive information on the geography, history, governmental structure, economy, cultural diversity, peoples, religion, and culture of Andorra."—Provided by publisher.
  Includes bibliographical references and index.
  ISBN 978-0-7614-3122-0
1.   Andorra—Juvenile literature. I. Title.

DC924.A84 2009

946.7'd—dc22   2007040356

Printed in China
7 6 5 4 3 2 1

CONTENTS

Street cafés along the Valira River.

The Pal ski area in the Pyrenees in Andorra.

INTRODUCTION

CARTOGRAPHERS HAVE DRAFTED MAPS of Europe that have defined the boundaries of Andorra and validated its political existence for almost twelve centuries. Yet many of the world's citizens do not know where Andorra is located. Isolated in the Pyrenees Mountains, the country has long escaped the interest of most outsiders. Andorra was ruled by two co-princes who essentially governed the country as a feudal state. Most of its citizens back then lived simple lives focused on raising livestock and growing a few grains, vegetables, and fruits.

In the middle of the 20th century Andorra suddenly exploded from a traditional rural society to a dynamic urban and economic showcase. Commerce, banking, and tourism replaced subsistence agriculture in a healthy free-market economy. A new constitution created an independent parliamentary democracy that allowed Andorra to take its legitimate place in the international community. It is a country blessed with a bounty of natural beauty and a nation of hardworking, genuine, and compassionate citizens. Andorra's future is bright, and it is rapidly erasing its reputation as an unknown in international relations and winning the admiration of all those who visit and learn more about this jewel in the Pyrenees.

GEOGRAPHY

ANDORRA IS A SMALL, LANDLOCKED nation nestled in the eastern Pyrenees Mountains, between France and Spain. Considered one of Europe's microstates, along with Liechtenstein, Luxembourg, Malta, Monaco, San Marino, and Vatican City, Andorra's total area is 175 square miles (453 square km), approximately two and a-half times larger than Washington, D.C.

A LAND OF MOUNTAINS AND VALLEYS

The country's geography is dominated by two major physical features: mountains and valleys. A portion of the Pyrenees Mountains covers much of the land surface and helps make Andorra one of the most unique countries in Europe. Tectonic activity that took place between 100 and 150 million years ago resulted in intense pressure and uplifting of the Earth's crust, contributing to the creation of the Pyrenees. Igneous and metamorphic rocks make up the dominant geology of Andorra. Different types of igneous granites are especially common, as are metamorphic gneisses, schists, and slates. All of these rocks have played a role in the construction of traditional Andorran buildings, especially the use of granite for external walls. Black slate, called *pissarra negra* in the native Catalan language, is used for roofing in most construction.

Above: **Black slate is a rock that is commonly used as roofing material in Andorra.**

Opposite: **Towering snow covered peaks of the Pyrenees Mountains.**

7

GEOGRAPHY

Special recognition Andorra can claim based on its physical characteristics include the highest average elevation of any country in Europe, at 6,548 feet (1,996 m), and the continent's highest capital city, Andorra la Vella, at 3,540 feet (1,079 m). The craggy, mountainous landscape produces 65 peaks of more than 6,560 feet (2,000 m) and one peak, Pic de Coma Pedrosa, near the northwestern border with France and Spain, of 9,652 feet (2,942 m). This rugged mountain landscape has been both a blessing and a curse. For centuries the rugged terrain served to isolate Andorra from the rest of the world. Recently, however, the physical charm of its many mountains and valleys is helping to attract millions of tourists each year for outdoor summer activities and winter skiing.

The valleys of Andorra are essentially a part of one drainage basin containing three major river branches and six open basins.

LAKE ENGOLASTERS

The most popular lake in Andorra is nestled in a small, oblong glacial depression.

Lake Engolasters is a short 20-minute drive from the nation's capital, Andorra la Vella. Located at 5,250 feet (1,600 m) above sea level, it provides a perfect escape from the noise and air pollution common in the capital city.

The lake's waters are a deep blue, and the shore is lined by velvet green meadows and stately pine trees. In the background the high, snow-clad peaks of the Pyrenees delight visitors with remarkable vistas. Visitors may picnic, fish for trout, or take a 2-mile (3.2-km) hike along the shoreline.

Lake Engolasters also plays an important role in the production of energy for Andorra. Water collected from the East Valira and Madriu rivers is moved through an underground tunnel to the lake. From the lake the water is funneled into a pipeline, through which it flows into Andorra's major hydroelectricity plant, near Encamp. This clean, renewable source of energy provides approximately 15 percent of Andorra's electricity.

The Valira River (Riu Valira) and its two major tributaries, the North Valira (Valira del Nord) and the East Valira (Valira d'Orient), create a deeply incised Y-shape in the mountainous landscape of Andorra. The North Valira begins in the northwestern corner of the country and flows south to meet the East Valira at Escaldes. There, the two tributaries join to form the Valira, which flows into the Segre River in Spain and later into the Ebro before its waters enter the Mediterranean Sea.

The valleys created by glaciers nearly 2,000 feet (610 m) thick during the last Ice Age are spectacular, with sheer rock cliffs rising almost vertically for hundreds of feet. The valley bottoms provide small areas of flat land and are the main sites of human settlement. Almost all of Andorra's population is located in small towns and villages strung out like pearls on a necklace along the course of the three major rivers.

RIVERS AND LAKES

The Valira River and its many tributaries have played an important role in the development of Andorra. The river valleys have provided the only access to Andorra both in the past and in the present. There are no airports or railroad networks in the entire country. Access to Andorra requires following the course of the Valira River from Spain or the East Valira from France. To penetrate the interior of the country by road, it is necessary to follow the river tributaries to their sources in the high mountains.

The rivers have also provided irrigation water for small tobacco, grain, and vegetable fields. Prior to the use of electricity, small industries, including textiles and iron forges, utilized water power by harnessing the rivers' waters to operate waterwheels. Today the rivers are the major source of

Opposite: **The city of Sant Juliá de Lória nestled along the banks of the Valira River in a narrow glacial valley.**

Below: **Andorra is dependepent on its rivers and streams to irrigate its crops.**

water for local needs. Andorra la Vella, the largest city in Andorra, and Escaldes-Engordany draw much of their water from the clean, high-quality waters of the Madriu River.

Andorra is blessed with more than 60 small lakes of glacial origin that dot the mountain landscape. The largest of these lakes is Lake Juclar, which covers approximately 70 acres (28 ha). The beautiful natural lakes serve as major tourist attractions during the summer months for thousands of tourists who have a desire to commune with nature in an unspoiled environment. The water from some of the lakes is so pure and sweet that it can be safely consumed by drinking it directly.

There are many small glacial lakes scattered throughout the mountains of Andorra.

One additional water resource that contributes to significant tourist revenue for Andorra is the country's hot springs. The city of Escaldes, whose name is derived from the Latin term *calidae*, meaning a warm water source, has long been recognized as the site of one of the hottest thermal springs in Europe, with water temperatures of 154°F (68°C). The springs were originally used in the 15th century to provide hot water for washing and dying wool in a small textile industry. Today a modern tourist complex called Caldea draws hundreds of visitors each day to the hot springs.

The city of Escaldes is located in a narrow valley where the East and North Valira rivers meet to form the Valira River.

CALDEA

Caldea is Europe's largest hot springs spa, covering more than 64,584 square feet (6,000 sq m) with indoor and outdoor facilities. There are warm water lagoons, saunas, whirlpool baths, Indo-Roman baths, waterfalls, warm marble slabs for massages, and many other stress- and fatigue-reducing treatments. The interior accommodations are housed in an ultramodern blue glass structure that dominates the skyline of Escaldes. In winter guests can settle into outdoor pools filled with steaming thermal waters and view majestic, snow-covered peaks surrounding the city, which are just a short distance from the complex.

CLIMATE

Andorra has one of the most pleasant climates in the world. The entire country is characterized by a high mountain climate with a Mediterranean influence. The average annual minimum temperature is 28°F (–2°C), and the average annual maximum temperature is 75°F (24°C). Winters are cool but not harsh, except at the highest elevations. Summers are mild to warm, with clear skies and bright sunshine. In fact, Andorra's mountains and valleys are bathed in sunshine for more than half the year. On rare occasions Arctic fronts from northern Europe push into the Pyrenees with high winds and cold temperatures producing wind chill indexes below 0°F (-17.8°C).

On April 7, 1718, the worst avalanche in Andorran history occurred. Five people were killed, as were 30 cows, 23 mules, and 7 other animals.

The Pyrenees Mountains covered in snow created by warm moist air cooling as it rises over the mountains.

The Arinsal ski resort. Much of Andorra's tourism industry is dependent on the winter snows that fall from November to March or April.

Precipitation is moderate, averaging between 30 and 35 inches (762 and 890 mm) each year. Moisture-laden air masses from both the Atlantic Ocean and the Mediterranean Sea rise over the Pyrenees, producing lifting and the resultant precipitation. During winter the precipitation falls as snow, beginning in November and continuing into late March or early April. These winter snows are critical to the tourist industry, as they attract hundreds of thousands of skiers to what is arguably the best skiing in the Pyrenees.

FLORA AND FAUNA

In a mountainous environment such as Andorra's, the distribution of different species of plants is essentially a response to elevation. In the lowest elevations of southern Andorra, near Sant Julià de Lòria, the

Mediterranean influence is the strongest. Hence chestnut and walnut trees can be found, as well as a variety of pine trees. Along the river valleys, wild grasses and flowers are abundant, including blue gentian, red rhododendron, and the national flower of Andorra, the poet's narcissus or pheasant's eye. Higher up the mountain slopes the ground cover changes mostly to pine and fir trees until the timberline is reached. At this elevation the trees disappear, and only alpine meadows exist. Once the winter snows melt, the meadows are covered in grass, violets, daisies, moss, and wild blackberries and strawberries. During summer, herds of sheep and cattle are moved to the meadows for grazing.

The fauna of Andorra is also affected by altitudinal zones. The Pyrenean chamois (isard), ptarmigan, and lammergeier are all found at higher

The national flower of Andorra is the pheasant's eye, which is more commonly known as the poet's narcissus.

THE ISARD

The Pyrenean chamois, commonly called the isard by native Andorrans, is one of the national symbols of Andorra. It is a member of the antelope family and is usually found on the high meadows or rocky slopes at elevations between 6,500 and 9,650 feet (1,980 and 2,940 m). The animal is relatively small with a length of 3 to 4 feet (1 to 1.2 m) and a height of 2 to 2.5 feet (0.61 to 0.76 m). A full-grown adult isard weighs between 50 and 90 pounds (22.7 and 41 kg).

The isard's hooves have sharp edges that permit it to cling to steep mountain slopes. The animal can run at breakneck speeds on some of the most difficult terrain in the Pyrenees. It is a cunning animal that is very suspicious of humans, which makes it difficult to hunt. However, native Andorrans have hunted the isard for centuries.

Since the number of isards in Andorra is limited, the government restricts the hunting season to one week each fall. This event is known as the *caça de izard*, or the hunt of the isard. During the short hunting season mostly male hunters trek into the high mountains, where they camp and hunt for the full week. The hunt is as much about male bonding and camaraderie as it is about bagging an isard.

elevations. The lammergeier is a magnificent member of the vulture family that stands more than 40 inches (1 m) in height, with a wingspan of nearly 10 feet (3 m). Unfortunately, this unique bird only survives in small numbers and has been placed on the endangered species list. Farther down the mountains, squirrels, wild boar, and capercaillie (European grouse) are more common. At the lowest elevations fox, partridge, hare, and many other species abound.

Sport fishing is very popular in Andorra's rivers and glacial lakes. Trout are plentiful and delicious because of the high quality and purity of the water. In addition, the federal government operates a large fish hatchery that ensures regular restocking of lakes and rivers.

A lammergeier, also known as a bearded vulture, is an endangered species.

HISTORY

THE HISTORY OF ANDORRA IS NOT WELL documented and, in fact, scholars have probably conducted more historical research on Andorra in the past fifteen years than during the previous fifteen centuries combined. Very few major historical studies discuss Andorra, and the country has produced only a small number of historical scholars. Andorra did not have a university until 1997, and the newly established Institute of Andorran Studies has accomplished much of the current historical research. Scholars from the Institute are combing the ancient archives of the Catholic Church as well as libraries in Spain and France in an attempt to document the fascinating past of this small nation. The National Archives of Andorra, soon to be housed in a Frank Gehry-designed building in La Massana, also shelters priceless documents related to the foundation of Andorra and its historical quest for peace. These documents are a prime resource for historians wishing to study the Middle Ages and Andorran history.

EARLY HUMAN OCCUPATION

Recent investigations of an archaeological site on the Valira River near La Margineda have established the presence of humans dating back to 10,500 B.C., a date confirmed by using radiocarbon dating on bone fragments. The Valira River plain near Sant Julià de Lòria offered an excellent environment for settlement, and small groups lived in this region during the Neolithic Period. In 1959, the 4,000-year-old skeletal remains of a woman were discovered.

The long winters with heavy snowfall were not conducive to permanent settlement by early humans, so most groups were probably nomadic, only remaining in the area for short periods of time. Some evidence suggests that the Basques may have occupied portions of Andorra before moving to the western Pyrenees. The Andosinos, an Iberian people,

Opposite: **Andorrans believe that in the early 9th century Emperor Charlemagne declared Andorra to be a sovereign state.**

were most likely the first permanent settlers. They were mentioned by the noted Greek historian Polybius when he described Hannibal's expedition through the Pyrenees Mountains in 219 B.C. to 218 B.C.

ROMAN INFLUENCE

Andorra was part of the Roman Empire, and while Rome paid little attention to this small outpost, the relationship had a long-term impact on the country. Catalan, the official language of Andorra, is a Latin-based Romance language. Roman law still dictates much of the foundation of the Andorran legal system. After the fall of the Roman Empire, the Visigoths passed through the valleys of Andorra but showed little interest in establishing a permanent presence.

THE MOORS

In 711, the Moorish general Tarik ibn Ziyad crossed the Strait of Gibraltar and led a series of battles through which he conquered the Iberian Peninsula in a few months. The Muslim Moors then pushed across the Pyrenees and into France. One of the many routes they took was through Andorra, where they received a hostile reception from the largely Christian Andorrans. While the Andorrans resisted the invasion, their small numbers had little effect on the rapidly moving Moorish cavalry and infantry. Finally, in 732, as the Moors moved north, they were defeated by Charles Martel at the Battle of Poitiers. The process of expelling the Moors from Europe began at this point, and it took more than 750 years before the last Moorish kingdom, Granada, fell. Emperor Charlemagne played a significant role in defeating the Moors.

At this time in history, facts become clouded with legend regarding Charlemagne's influence on Andorra. Undocumented legend holds that Charlemagne, out of gratitude to the Andorrans for their resistance against the Moors, declared them a sovereign people in 788. His decree is said to have established the early boundaries of the country of Andorra. Many Andorrans believe that Charlemagne created an official document in the early ninth century that legally established Andorra's independence. The document is known as the Carta de Fundació d'Andorra. For centuries the document was locked in a special cabinet in the city of Andorra la Vella. The charter has since been moved to a vault in the archives of the bishop of Urgell, one of Andorra's co-princes. The document has been viewed by only a few individuals, and many historians currently believe that the charter was forged by the Andorrans to prevent France or Spain from absorbing the small nation into their national territory. The affection that the Andorrans continue to hold for the emperor Charlemagne is apparent in their national anthem, which was officially adopted in 1914.

HISTORICAL RECOGNITION

In 839 the first reference to the "Valleys of Andorra" appeared in a document titled

Act of Consecration and Assignment of the Cathedral of Seu d'Urgell. This document certified the inclusion of the six parishes of the Valleys of Andorra, with all of their churches and possessions, to the diocese of Urgell in Spain. The content of the document was reaffirmed four years later by the grandson of Charlemagne, King Charles the Bald, when he gave the Valleys of Andorra to Sunifred I, the count of Urgell and Cerdanya.

The principal political authority over Andorra remained with the counts of Urgell until 1007, when Count Ermengol I transferred half of Andorra's territory to the bishops of Urgell. In 1133, Count Ermengol IV gave control over all of Andorra's territory to the bishops of Urgell. Over the next century and a half, power struggles between the Church and the nobles, as well as some strategic marriages, placed control of Andorra in the House of Foix, in France. Bickering and conflict between the House of Foix and the Spanish bishops eventually led to discussions and a compromise that allowed both sides to share in the governance of Andorra.

THE ANDORRAN NATIONAL ANTHEM

The Great Charlemagne
> The Great Charlemagne, my Father, from the Saracens liberated me,
> And from heaven he gave me life of Meritxell the great mother.
> I was born a princess, a maiden neutral between two nations.
> I am the only remaining daughter of the Carolingian empire
> Believing and free for eleven centuries, believing and free I will be
> The laws of the land be my tutors, and my defender Princess!

THE PAREATGES

The creation of the modern Principality of Andorra dates to 1278 and 1288, with the signing of two agreements termed pareatges. The first pareatge created the concept of a co-principality ruled by two co-princes, the bishop of Urgell and the count of Foix. Each co-prince was given equal rights over the administration of Andorra. The Andorrans were required to pay a small annual fee, the *questia*, in alternate years to each of the co-princes. The second pareatge reaffirmed the contents of the original agreement and settled some minor differences between the two co-princes. Thus, the first government, with two heads of state, was created. The agreement served the Andorrans well for more than 700 years, as this tiny nation weathered centuries of conflict in the region while perched high in the Pyrenees Mountains between France and Spain.

The status of the bishop of Urgell as co-prince of Andorra has not changed since 1278. However, on the French side of the border the position of co-prince has changed substantially. Arranged marriages for

There has never been a female co-princess during Andorra's history.

THE FRENCH REVOLUTION'S IMPACT ON ANDORRA

The one exception to the continuity of the co-princes' administration of Andorra occurred during the French Revolution. The French revolutionaries rejected the pareatge and *questia* as being feudal in nature and terminated the rights of the French king as co-prince over Andorra in 1793. This action caused great concern in Andorra, whose population feared that the delicate balance of power and their neutrality might be threatened. In 1806, the Andorrans successfully petitioned Emperor Napoleon I to restore the status of the French head of state as a co-prince of Andorra.

political purposes resulted in the viscounts of Béarn assuming the title of coprince of Andorra. When Henry IV of Béarn became king of France, the title was passed to the French head of state, where it remains today. The newly elected president of France, Nicolas Sarkozy, is currently France's co-prince of Andorra.

THE MIDDLE AGES

Over the next few centuries life in Andorra changed imperceptibly. The population of sturdy mountain people seldom exceeded more than 3,000 to 4,000 until the 20th century. Few outsiders ventured into Andorra because there were no roads to provide easy access to the country. Bayard Taylor, a noted author and travel writer, claimed in the year 1867 that he was the first American ever to visit Andorra.

Protected by their neutrality and isolation, the Andorrans were satisfied to live in a peaceful, if not prosperous, society. Their homes were constructed from local rock and covered with natural slate roofs. They grew grains and vegetables wherever they could find a flat spot with soil and grazed their livestock in the alpine meadows during the summers. They negotiated favorable trade agreements with both of their powerful neighbors, France and Spain, and their work ethic and friendly nature earned the respect of the few individuals who visited Andorra.

The Middle Ages were a great moment for architecture in Andorra. The simple but extraordinary Romanesque churches were built with the help of artists inspired by the buildings in Lombardy in northern Italy. Magnificent Romanesque frescoes such as those of Santa Coloma, recently recovered by the government of Andorra from Germany, where they had ended up after World War II, are outstanding examples of this artistic period in European history. A few sturdy but graceful stone Romanesque bridges still dot the rivers of Andorra.

The most significant event affecting Andorra during the Middle Ages was the establishment of the Council of the Land in 1419. Representatives of some of the leading families petitioned the co-princes to allow them to create a democratically elected body of representatives that would serve as spokesmen for the people and be given the authority to conduct the day-to-day affairs of the principality. Both co-princes, Bishop Francesc de Tovia of Urgell and John I, Count of Foix, agreed to support the creation of the Council of the Land. This action created one of the oldest parliaments in Europe and served as the forerunner of today's General Council. While this process sparked the beginning of democratic governance in Andorra, only the male heads of households from the leading families could vote or serve on the Council of the Land.

THE 19TH CENTURY

The process of democratization was given a big boost in 1866 with passage of the New Reform, which was approved by both co-princes. The New Reform expanded the right to vote to all male heads of

Opposite: **French president Nicolas Sarkozy is now the co-prince of Andorra.**

households over 25 years of age, not just those from leading families. It also increased the responsibilities of the Council of the Land and the administrators of the parish governments.

The Industrial Revolution arrived in Andorra in the mid-1800s with the opening of more iron mines and small, independent forges. However, the iron industry was short-lived because of the low-grade iron ores available locally and transportation difficulties. Smuggling, which had always taken place in Andorra, expanded into a full-blown economic asset for Andorrans. The Carlist wars in Spain, from 1832 to 1840, sparked a substantial increase in smuggling, as weapons and supplies moved from France to Spain, and refugees from Spain moved to France through Andorra.

A NEW DAWN

The 20th century brought changes in Andorra that completely altered the nature of the country's traditional society. In 1913, a road link to Spain was completed, providing thousands of Spaniards access to the principality. In addition, road construction throughout the major valleys was initiated, and a highway connection to France was completed in 1935. Both France and Spain initiated postal services for Andorra, and the first ski resort opened in 1934. A new hydroelectricity plant at Encamp began generating electricity in 1935, and a radio station went on the air in the same year. Suddenly, Andorra was no longer the isolated, forgotten principality of the Pyrenees.

After 1933, political changes occurred rapidly. All adult male citizens over twenty-five years of age were given the right to vote, and women voted for the first time in 1970. In 1952, Andorra signed its first international agreement by accepting the principles of the Geneva

Agreement on intellectual property. Meanwhile, the co-princes were pushing the General Council to modernize the political and social structures of Andorra in preparation for the country to receive international recognition as a constitutional state. An executive council and head of government were established in 1981, providing Andorra with an administrative branch of government. In 1990, formal work was begun on drafting a new constitution that would provide for a constitutional democracy in Andorra. In March 1993, three-quarters of Andorran voters approved the new constitution. Later in the same year Andorra joined the United Nations as a full member, with the sovereign powers of the nation vested in the citizens of Andorra. The bishop of Urgell and the president of France remain as heads of state and coprinces, but serve largely ceremonial roles.

THE FIRST KING OF ANDORRA

In 1933 a conflict between the General Council and young Andorran men over voting rights resulted in the dismissal of the General Council. The General Council refused to accept this action, and months of unrest and struggle ensued. These disputes led to one of the most unusual political events in Andorran history. Baron Boris de Skossyreff, the self-proclaimed count of Orange, from the Netherlands, claimed himself to be King Boris I of Andorra. The General Council, seeking to establish a constitutional monarchy, accepted Skossyreff as their first king. The bishop of Urgell was not amused at this attempt to interfere with his political power in Andorra and sent Spanish civil guards to arrest Skossyreff. Skossyreff was brought before a judge in Barcelona, spent time in a Madrid prison, and was exiled to Portugal. Later investigations proved that King Boris I was a fraud, his claim to be a Dutch count totally false.

GOVERNMENT

TO ANDORRANS, THE DOCUMENTED ORIGINS of a state in need of governance date to 839. On this date the six parishes of the Valleys of Andorra were assigned as possessions of the diocese of Urgell in a document titled the *Act of Consecration* and *Assignment of the Cathedral of Seu d'Urgell*. Over the next four centuries a series of nobles and religious leaders on both the Spanish and French sides of the Pyrenees argued over the right to govern Andorra. In reality, little governance was provided to the small population of Andorrans, who lived in isolated valleys, and contact with their feudal lords was rare and inconsistent.

In 1278 and 1288, two agreements called pareatges were signed, which gave the power to govern Andorra to the bishop of Urgell in Spain and the count of Foix in France as equal co-princes. The Andorrans viewed this action as an acceptable solution that would allow them to maintain

Left: **The flag of Andorra.**

Opposite: **The Casa de la Vall, Andorra's seat of government, is located in Andorra's capital, Andorra La Vella.**

The 1993 constitution has 107 articles.

their neutrality while providing them with security. They agreed to pay a small tax, the *questia*, to both co-princes and proceeded to live in isolation over the next seven centuries.

SMALL STEPS TOWARD DEMOCRACY

During the Middle Ages the economy and social organization of the Principality of Andorra served as an excellent example of medieval feudalism. The first step toward democracy was taken in 1419, when the co-princes approved the formation of the Council of the Land, a primitive form of parliament. While the Council was authorized and empowered to deal with local political needs, it was far from being a truly democratic institution. The only people allowed to serve on the Council and vote in the election of Council members were third-generation males over 25 years of age who were heads of households from the elite families of Andorra. The leading wealthy families held this dominant position regarding internal political decisions until the passage of the New Reform, in 1866. The reform allowed all male heads of households over 25 years of age the right to vote and serve on the Council, if elected. Democracy was creeping into Andorran politics at a snail's pace, but progress was being made. In 1933, after raucous demonstrations by young Andorrans had shaken the conservative, elderly members of the Council, universal suffrage was granted to all male citizens over 25. Women would have to wait until 1970 for the right to vote, and in 1985, the voting age was lowered to 18 for all citizens. After more than a millennium of political domination by outsiders, Andorra was ready to step across the threshold into a sovereign parliamentary democracy.

THE TRANSITION TO FULL SOVEREIGNTY

The next significant step on the road toward democracy was made by an unlikely player. In the late 1970s, the Andorran parliament issued directives for political reform. In 1981, the co-princes suggested that it was time to form an executive branch of government to speed the movement toward self-governance. An executive council was formed, with six ministers who were directed to govern Andorra, while the co-princes still preserved the ultimate power.

In 1990, new pressure from the Council of Europe stimulated an interest in the completion of a constitution. The Council suggested that if Andorra had any hope of full integration into Europe's core institutions, the country would have to have a modern constitution. A committee of representatives selected by the co-princes, the General Council, and the newly formed Executive Council started work on a draft immediately. The draft was presented to the public in March 1993. Three-quarters of all eligible voters cast their ballots in the constitutional referendum, and the document was approved by 75 percent of those who voted.

The constitution provided for three branches of government represented by executive, legislative, and judicial divisions to maintain the proper checks and balances of a stable democracy. The co-princes were kept as heads of state, but their responsibilities were significantly reduced and became largely ceremonial in nature, as befits some parliamentary monarchies. The new government was allowed to shape its own foreign policy and participate in international relations. On July 28, 1993, Andorra was admitted as the 184th member of the United Nations, where it has distinguished itself on the issues of human rights, development, and international terrorism.

THE STRUCTURE OF GOVERNMENT

Officially, Andorra is still considered a principality with two co-princes as heads of state. The French president, newly elected Nicolas Sarkozy, and Bishop Joan Enric Vives i Sicilía of Urgell have equal powers in minor areas of government decision making and operate in ways similar to other constitutional monarchs in parliamentary monarchies in which they reign but do not rule. They have the authority to approve international treaties with France and Spain as well as those that deal with Andorra's internal security, defense, boundary disputes, and judicial and penal cooperation. Both co-princes are represented by delegates in Andorra la Vella, the nation's capital. In the past the French co-prince had seldom visited Andorra, while the bishop of Urgell had been a frequent visitor as much for religious reasons as political purposes. The Andorrans view the co-princes in a similar fashion as the British or the Canadians view their queen. After more than seven centuries, holding on to this tradition provides a kind of emotional security that is not easy for the Andorrans to give up. It also helps provide a balance of power in a small nation tucked between two much larger neighbors.

The executive branch of government is headed by the *cap de govern* (prime minister) and his cabinet. The prime minister is elected by a majority of the members of the General Council after the national elections are held (every four years). The prime minister then appoints the cabinet ministers, who form the Govern, or cabinet. Together, the prime minister and Executive Council are responsible for shaping domestic and foreign policy, developing a budget, and exercising the regulatory powers provided by the constitution. The prime minister is restricted to two consecutive four-year terms in office. Albert Pintat Santolària was elected as prime minister in April 2005 and will serve until the April-May elections of 2009. In May 2007, in an attempt to streamline his Executive Council, he compressed his cabinet by reducing the number of ministers from eleven to nine.

The legislative branch is the oldest division of the government. It traces its beginnings to the founding of the Council of the Land in 1419. It has evolved into a 28-member unicameral parliament currently named the Consell General de las Valls (General Council of the Valleys). Members of the General Council are elected to four- year terms during national elections. Each of the seven parishes elects two members from within its boundaries. The other fourteen members are elected from the entire national constituency. After each election the General Council chooses a speaker (sindic general) and a deputy speaker (Subsindic

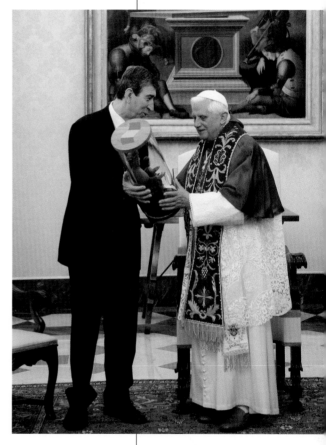

Above: **Prime minister of Andorra, Albert Pintat Santolária (*left*) meets with Pope Benedict XVI (*right*).**

Opposite: **The bishop of Urgell co-prince of Andorra, Joan Enric Vives i Sicilía.**

35

General) to carry out the decisions of the council. The constitution requires that at least one representative from each of the seven parishes be present before the council conducts official business. The General Council works closely with the Executive Council in developing new legislation, forming policy, making budget adjustments, and representing the interests of its constituents and the nation as a whole.

The constitution of 1993 also provided for a major reform of the judicial system that was previously administered in the name of the co-princes.

Andorra's 28-member parliament currently meets in this chamber in the Casa de la Vall, located in Andorra la Vella, the nation's capital.

Legal matters today are conducted on behalf of Andorran citizens. The highest legal council in the land is the Consell Superior de la Justica (Supreme Council of Justice). This council oversees and administers the entire justice system of Andorra. There is also the Andorran Supreme Court, or the Tribunal Constitucional (Constitutional Court). There are five members of this court, each of whom must be an Andorran national who is over 25 years of age and well experienced in the practice of law. One member is appointed by each co-prince, one by the sindic general (speaker of General Council), one by the prime minister, and one by the magistrates. The court's decisions are irreversible and cannot be appealed. The Supreme Council of Justice appoints the leaders of the three lower courts and keeps a watchful eye on court proceedings and attorney behavior. The three lower courts, the Tribunal of Judges, Tribunal of Courts, and the Supreme Tribunal of Justice, make up the remainder of the judicial system and deal with civil and criminal cases as well as legal interpretations of the constitution. Lower-court decisions may be appealed to the Andorran Supreme Court.

The Andorran flag has three vertical bands of equal size. The first is blue, the middle is yellow, and the third is red. The Andorran coat of arms is located in the center of the yellow band.

POLITICAL PARTIES AND VOTER PARTICIPATION

Political parties were illegal in Andorra until the 1993 constitution lifted the ban, although one party was formed in 1979 and was quietly tolerated. In the 2005 elections, three different political parties sent representatives to parliament, with the Liberal Party capturing 14 seats, the Social Democratic Party capturing 12 seats, and the Democratic Center Party capturing 2 seats. The major parties are affiliated with such international political groups as Liberal International, the Socialist International, and the Center Democrat International and are within the mainstream of similar parties in Europe. From 1997 to 2005, the

THE SOMATÉN

Andorra does not have an army, navy, or air force. There has not been a war in Andorra since its formation and establishment of boundaries, in A.D. 839. However, through the ages the country has been defended by a group known as the Somatén. By tradition, each family in Andorra assigned one male member of the family, usually the father or oldest son, to represent the family in the Somatén. Each individual member was required to have a rifle and an adequate supply of bullets. Every individual was an officer, but no member wore a uniform. The Somatén had no women. Because Andorra never went to war, the Somatén engaged primarily in ceremonial functions at national celebrations or acted as volunteers to maintain order after natural disasters, such as avalanches and floods. In 1929, a national police force was established, with seven members. Today the National Police Force employs 250 men and women, and the status of the Somatén is largely in limbo.

Liberal Party governed with an absolute majority. It still governs, but with a reduced majority.

In the most recent election about 83 percent of eligible voters went to the polls, illustrating a widespread interest across Andorra in participation in the democratic process. Since earning the right to vote in 1970, the role of women in government has grown rapidly. The current parliament has eight female members, twice the number of women who served on the previous General Council. The subsindic of parliament (deputy speaker) is a woman, Bernadeta Gaspà Bringueret. The current prime minister's cabinet has three female members out of a total of nine ministers, including the ministers of foreign affairs, education, and health.

LOCAL ADMINISTRATION

Each of Andorra's seven parishes (Andorra la Vella, Canillo, Encamp, La Massana, Ordino, Sant Julià de Lòria, and Escaldes-Engordany) maintains its own local government, with powers guaranteed by the 1993 constitution. Members of the local administrative bodies referred to as *comuns* are elected during national elections. Each comu determines the size of its council, based on population. Most councils have between 10 and 14 members. The councils then select a *cónsol major* (mayor) and a *cónsol menor* (deputy mayor) to lead the parish.

The *comuns* are public corporations with full legal status, and they control regulatory power over ordinances and regulations of the parishes. The local governments are quite powerful, as they have control over large blocks of communal land that is sometimes a source of substantial revenue, such as when ski resorts are developed on it. The *comuns* are also responsible for conducting regular censuses, managing electoral procedures in the parish, performing local planning, creating and maintaining public services, managing the use of natural resources, and other functions. Financial assistance through the transfer of funds from the general budget of the state helps ensure monetary security for the parishes.

The comuns are responsible for supplying water to each parish. This particular tank serves the parish of Sant Juliá de Lória.

ECONOMY

TRACING THE ECONOMIC DEVELOPMENT of Andorra requires an analysis of two distinct time frames. The first part stretches over more than 1,100 years, from 839 until 1950, while the second part involves a period of less than 60 years. During the first stage Andorra was isolated from the rest of the world because of its remote, mountainous location and a lack of transportation connections. It possessed only small amounts of natural resources and scarce areas of arable land, and the country was under the political control of individuals who were not particularly interested in the development of their feudal territory. The economy that developed under these circumstances was basic and traditional.

The main source of livelihood was agriculture, which was largely subsistence in nature rather than commercial. Grains, vegetables, and fruit were raised on small plots of land along the narrow plains of the major river valleys. Livestock, mostly sheep, were grazed on the high alpine meadows during the summer months. During the 18th century tobacco became an important crop that led to the development of widespread smuggling. Andorrans of this time period considered smuggling to be a lawful activity, and some families acquired considerable wealth from it over time. The locations of the trails used for smuggling were a closely guarded secret, and Andorrans moved freely across both the Spanish and French borders. These skills served the country well during the Carlist wars and Francisco Franco's dictatorship in Spain, and during both world wars. The establishment of road connections from Spain in 1913 and France in 1935 led to changes that would spawn a new economic era after 1950.

DRAMATIC GROWTH

As the population of Andorra increased from approximately 6,000 inhabitants in 1950 to more than 75,000 in 2005, economic growth was

Opposite: **The tourism industry has seen an increase in the construction of facilities, such as resorts and hotels, to accomodate the growing number of visitors to Andorra.**

explosive. Today Andorra has a strongly developed free-market economy heavily dependent on the services sector. In 2005, the annual growth in economic activity was a healthy 3.5 percent. A per-capita income of $37,000 a year places Andorra above the average for all of Europe and ahead of its two larger neighbors, Spain and France. At the same time wise fiscal management in both the private and public sector has kept the rate of inflation around 3 percent.

The central government has played an essential role in creating a healthy economic environment since Andorra became a totally sovereign nation, in 1993. Each successive administration has limited the growth and expense of government services while keeping debt at a minimum. As a result, the interest spent on the national debt is small, thereby freeing up capital for continued investment and development.

THE SERVICE SECTOR

Tourism, with a recorded all-time high of 11.6 million tourists, in 2004, is primarily responsible for the growth of the service sector. Retail sales, skiing, hiking, and other recreational specialties are the main attractions for foreign visitors.

More than 2,000 specialized duty-free shops offer merchandise from all over the world, including alcohol, tobacco products, high-fashion clothing, jewelry, electronics, sports equipment, perfume, specialty foodstuffs, and much more. Nearly 80 percent of all tourists are excursion tourists or day shoppers who arrive early in the mornings from Spain and France and return to their homes on the same day. They are attracted by prices that are at least 25 percent lower than those in their own countries and the absence of a sales tax. In addition, comparison shopping is easy, as most shops are concentrated in small areas. Another attraction is that the stores are open for long hours for 361 days each year. The only days the shops are closed are the four national holidays, when the government requires their closure.

WINTER SPORTS

Andorra has what is arguably the best skiing in the Pyrenees Mountains. The country has five separate ski resorts that have been consolidated

A shopping center in Andorra la Vella. Many of Andorra's visitors are from its neighboring countries that prefer to shop in Andorra due to its lower prices.

into three operations. They offer more than 186 miles (300 km) of ski runs, ranging from slopes designated green for beginners to black for the most skilled skiers. Even if nature does not cooperate during the ski season, more than 1,500 snow cannons make fresh snow over most of the runs. Andorra's reputation for having great skiing has grown, with resorts reporting more than 2.5 million ski days based on passes sold during the 2005 season. Skiers with a love of nature can cross-country ski in the lush pine forests of La Rabassa near Sant Julià de Lòria. Other winter enthusiasts can engage in snowboarding, snowshoeing, dog-

sledding, snow biking, and taking helicopter tours over the resorts.

SUMMER ACTIVITIES

The summer months attract a different type of tourist to Andorra. They are individuals who enjoy communing with nature, far from the hectic traffic congestion, air pollution, and noise of their home cities. Hiking is the most popular summer activity. One hiker has described 30 different hiking trails that cover a total distance of 198 miles (318.6 km). The paths are high quality, well maintained, and clearly marked. Many are paths that were previously used by livestock herders and smugglers. Hiking offers opportunities to engage in bird-watching, observe the alpine ecosystems with their beautiful flora, and improve personal health. Overnight camping is encouraged, and 26 comfortable stone refuges are scattered along the hiking paths and may be used, in most instances, free of charge. Other summer activities include mountain biking, trout fishing, horseback riding, and rock climbing.

Andorrans are well aware of the fact that the natural beauty of their country is one of its major attractions, and they are committed to preserving the fragile mountain environment.

The government's new Andorra 2020 Program stresses the need for strict environmental management to monitor and develop the tourist industry.

BANKING AND FINANCE

Andorra's financial sector has become one of the most promising developments in the principality. The financial sector has rapidly attained a reputation for providing quality professional services, with its significant monetary resources and superior management. The swift growth of the economy has encouraged investments in property and construction and helped fund a profitable real estate expansion.

Banks have also attracted large deposits from nonresidents, as the nonresident interest earnings have not been taxed. Bank security and secrecy have ensured that nonresident depositors have felt comfortable placing large sums of money in Andorran bank accounts. In fact, it is often stated that only three people know an individual's personal account number: the client, his banker, and God. Recently, pressure from European Union members has resulted in the institution of a modest withholding tax on EU residents' deposits. Most financial observers do not believe this action will have a great impact on banking in Andorra.

One unique aspect regarding financial matters is that Andorra does not have its own currency. In 2002, it adopted the euro as its official currency even though the nation is not a member of the European Union. Prior to the recent adoption of the euro, both the Spanish peseta and the French franc were widely used in Andorra.

INDUSTRY

Manufacturing has never played an important role in the Andorran economy. The lack of primary resources did not encourage the establishment of a strong industrial base, and a poor transportation system contributed substantially to a lack of development. Today less than 5 percent of the labor force is engaged in manufacturing, and most of these laborers work in paper and graphic arts, tobacco, food and beverage processing, and the distribution of electricity, gas, and water.

CONSTRUCTION

Since 1974, population and housing needs have more than tripled, and the number of both retail shops and storage warehouses for wholesale products has increased dramatically. Construction jobs currently account for 15 percent of the labor force. In recent years building permits for apartments have skyrocketed because most residents of Andorra, particularly foreigners, cannot afford the high cost of individual home ownership. Office buildings and shops have been a distant second in the number of building permits issued, and private home construction has accounted for a small percentage of permits.

Opposite: **One of many banks located in the financial district of Andorra la Vella.**

47

AGRICULTURE

At one time agriculture was the most important sector of the Andorran economy. Today agricultural jobs account for less than 0.5 percent of the labor force. Less than 2 percent of the nation's total land area can be farmed, and most of this acreage is broken into very small plots. A large farm in Andorra is about 37 acres (15 ha) in size. Almost all of the cultivated land is used to grow tobacco or wheat and grass, which are used for forage for livestock during the winter months. During summer, livestock are moved to the alpine meadows on the high-mountain communal lands for grazing on plants.

A building being constructed in Andorra la vella. Currently, 15 percent of Andorra's workforce is engaged in construction.

THE ANDORRAN TOBACCO STORY

Tobacco has played an important role in the Andorran economy for a long time. It was grown for local consumption for centuries. Then in the late 19th and early 20th centuries, a small number of tobacco factories was established to produce cigarettes, cigars, and snuff. Women, who worked long hours to supplement family income, did much of the labor in the factories. A considerable portion of the finished products were then smuggled across the borders into Spain and France.

After 1945, when Andorra began to open duty-free shops, many foreign tobacco companies wanted to sell their products in Andorra's shops. The clever Andorrans approved of the concept as long as the foreign companies were willing to buy the entire Andorran tobacco crop to make cigarettes in the factories they operated in Andorra. Because much of the tobacco grown in Andorra was produced in the valleys, where the mountains blocked sunlight for large portions of the day, Andorran tobacco had always been considered to be of inferior quality. A dilemma now faced the foreign tobacco companies. They were eager to have access to the large duty-free sales market, but they did not want to use low-grade Andorran tobacco. The solution was a unique compromise. The foreign tobacco companies imported high-grade tobacco to make their cigarettes. The Andorrans continued to grow their tobacco and were paid a premium price for each pound (kg). After the Andorran tobacco was weighed and the farmer paid, the tobacco was destroyed by burning the entire crop. This special arrangement is expected to end in the next three to four years.

ENVIRONMENT

HISTORICALLY ANDORRA HAS NOT BEEN faced with many of the environmental threats common in most nations since the beginnings of the Industrial Revolution. The country has no major fossil fuel reserves, smoke-belching factories, toxic chemical plants, or major mining operations. The few small iron-ore extraction operations that existed closed in the 19th century, and rock quarries ceased to function in the early 1970s. Because the population seldom exceeded 5,000 inhabitants before 1950, human pressure on the environment was minimal, except for deforestation and soil erosion caused by overgrazing.

Both of these problems had their roots in the land tenure system that had operated in the country for centuries. Eighty percent of all land in Andorra is under the control of the parish governments (*comuns*). The only property that the central government controls is the roads and highways, as well as the rivers and their banks. This fact has blocked the development of national policies regarding a number of environmental issues.

At the turn of the 20th century there was no executive branch of government to make policies. The parishes controlled and continue to control all of the forest resources within their boundaries. Forestry was one of the major economic activities that provided income to operate the local governments. Huge swaths of first-growth forests were cut down and exported primarily to Spain. Recognition of the potential danger to parish ecosystems resulted in the termination of timber extraction in the late 20th century. For a time parish residents were allowed to cut wood for their own use, which was mostly for fuel. All seven parishes recently established formal regulations that prohibit the cutting of trees in Andorra's forests. The most recent threat to the nation's forests has come from the extensive development of ski resorts, where large blocks of trees have been removed to create ski runs. Environmental

Opposite: **The Upper Ransol Valley in Andorra.**

organizations, such as the Greens of Andorra political party and the Andorran Association for the Defense of Nature, are challenging this damage to the mountain ecology.

In the past the other major environmental issue in Andorra was the overgrazing of communal alpine meadows. These communal lands were also managed by the parish governments, and the income from issuing grazing permits was necessary for the economic health of the parish. During the 1930s, as many as 60,000 sheep and goats grazed the high-mountain pastures for the summer months. Shepherds herded more than half of the livestock across the borders from Spain and France. The great numbers of animals led to overgrazing and plant destruction

Tracts of forests on Andorra's mountains are being cleared to make way for new developments catering to the increasing numbers of tourists to Andorra.

that increased the rate of soil erosion, clouding Andorra's streams with sediment. Today animals from France and Spain no longer enter Andorra, and local farmers graze fewer than 5,000 head of domestic livestock each year on the high meadows.

A sheep herdsman with his dog. Shepherds would herd their flocks to pastures like these for grazing.

NEW DANGERS

The rapid growth of the domestic population since 1950 and the influx of between 10 and almost 12 million tourists each year has created a new set of environmental challenges for Andorra. Air pollution, traffic congestion, solid waste disposal, wastewater treatment, and increased pressure on the nation's flora and fauna are all concerns that demand the attention of both the public and private sectors. The manner in which

In 2002, Andorra shut down an incinerator that was emitting 1,000 times the safe dioxin levels permitted by the European Union.

these challenges are met will determine the long-term ecological health of the country.

Currently, air pollution is the most serious environmental issue. Government surveys indicated that 4,381,802 vehicles entered Andorra in 2006, an average rate of 12,004 vehicles each day. The 60,000 cars owned by Andorrans also helped clog the roads and highways. With a limited number of roads serving the principality, traffic congestion can be almost intolerable. Vehicles move at a snail's pace in stop-and-go patterns, frustrating drivers and emitting harmful pollutants into the air. There is no place for the pollutants to escape, as the highways pass through steep-walled, narrow canyons. The most common complaint tourists register regarding their visit to Andorra is the poor air quality in the major urban areas, especially Andorra la Vella.

Air pollution and traffic congestion is a serious problem in Andorra.

Coming up with a solution to the air pollution problem is a high priority of the current government. One of the first projects encouraged by the new prime minister, Albert Pintat Santolària, was the creation of special bus lanes in the areas of highest traffic congestion. The lanes are restricted to buses only, which keeps the buses moving through the most heavily populated areas.

Because parking is at a premium, parking garages are being designed to be more environmentally friendly. Individual lights over each parking stall blink red if it is occupied and green if it is empty. This reduces the time spent searching for a space, which in turn reduces the pollution in the enclosed parking garages. As a means to conserve energy, many of the new garages also have motion detectors that automatically shut off the lights when no cars are moving in them.

Andorran traffic police are instrumental in ensuring that traffic flows smoothly.

The demands that tourists place on municipal services have also created additional environmental issues with wastewater treatment and solid-waste disposal. For many years, untreated sewage was allowed to flow into streams and rivers, making the water unsafe to drink. Since the expansion of the central government, programs have been established to correct this problem. New water-treatment plants now process more than 80 percent of all wastewater, and additional facilities are under construction. The goal is to have 100 percent of all wastewater treated within three years.

Solid-waste disposal also presents a significant challenge, as more than 11 million visitors each year create masses of solid waste (garbage). The government of Andorra recently began operating a new national cogeneration plant in Andorra la Vella using modern French technology. Cogeneration plants burn solid waste while generating electricity and using a sophisticated scrubber system to reduce harmful emissions into the air. The construction of additional cogeneration plants is currently under consideration. Recycling is also practiced to reduce solid waste and is considered a civic duty by the citizens of Andorra. Bright-colored containers at well-maintained collection sites for glass, aluminum, and cardboard are easily accessible around the country.

WILDLIFE

The flora and fauna of Andorra are under considerable pressure from increasing contact with humans. Their habitat is under attack by expanding road systems, expanding urban areas, and expanding tourist

Colorful recycling bins along the street in Andorra. Most Andorrans support efforts to save the environment.

developments, particularly the ski resorts. Because plants and animals are a significant part of the natural environment that attracts visitors to Andorra, their protection is essential. As a result the Ministry of Tourism and Environment recently established a new division employing agents as banders, who are similar to game wardens in the United States. These agents patrol the country in clearly marked four-wheel-drive vehicles, monitoring wildlife; assisting campers, hikers, and outdoor enthusiasts; and enforcing hunting and fishing regulations. The banders played an essential role when in 2005 and 2006, a pestivirus infected the isard herds and dramatically reduced their numbers. The division recommended reducing the one-week hunting season to three days in 2005 and closing the season in 2006. Since hunting the isard is a national tradition in Andorra, there was a huge protest from the hunters. However, because the herds recovered their numbers, the decision to prevent hunting was proved to be a good one. A large national fish hatchery has also ensured a successful trout restocking program in Andorra's rivers and lakes each year.

Banders have been employed by the government in a bid to protect and monitor Andorran wildlife.

SAVING THE BEST

A growing awareness of the need to protect the country's environment has led Andorrans to set aside some special ecological areas and to preserve them in their natural state. One of those areas is the La Rabassa Nature

The Andorrans established a national fish hatchery that ensures the number of fish set for release each year.

Reserve, near Sant Julià de Lòria. The reserve is popular for cross-country skiers who reject the fashionable downhill ski resorts to spend time quietly enjoying nature. The parish of Ordino closely reflects the historical past of Andorra and has established the Vall de Sorteny Natural Park to preserve the biodiversity of the region. The park has excellent hiking paths that allow visitors to observe more than 750 flowering plants during the spring and summer months.

The crown jewel of Andorra's protected areas is the Madriu-Perafita-Claror Valley. The valley was declared a United Nations World Heritage Site in 2004, and the protected area was enlarged in 2006. It is characterized by rugged cliffs formed by glaciers, high open pastures, steeply wooded valleys, and diverse flora and fauna. The site covers

9 percent of the total land area of Andorra and has no roads. Stone houses, terraced fields, and abandoned iron-smelting sites reflect a distant past in which humans had a more simple relationship with their natural environment. The minister of culture has protected this valley by issuing a decree based on the National Heritage Act. Despite legal action taken against the decree by landowners of the Madriu Valley and two of the four communes in which the protected area is located, the Constitutional Court ruled in favor of the minister in a well-publicized final decision on July 2007, which will help preserve the valley for decades to come.

Hotels in Andorra use plastic room keys that must be placed in a slot box inside the room to activate the electricity. When guests leave their rooms, they must remove their room keys. This action shuts off all electricity in their rooms, thereby conserving considerable amounts of energy.

INNOVATIONS IN AGRICULTURE

The outbreak of mad cow disease in Europe led to increased fears regarding beef consumption. While tourists to Andorra continued to demand beef in the many high-quality restaurants, they wanted assurances that the meat was safe. This created the opportunity for a special market for safe, organically raised cattle. The Associació de Ramaders (Andorran Farmers) organization was established to meet this need. Members of the organization raise cattle under extremely strict standards. All feed eaten by the animals must be free of preservatives and chemicals. Hay and grass consumed by the cattle must be grown using only manure for fertilizer. During the final fattening stage, males are separated from females and are placed in individual pens in temperature-controlled barns. Agricultural inspectors conduct tests on all cattle once a month to ensure that the animals are healthy and eating the proper diet. The cost of steaks from these organically raised animals is high, but customers are happy to buy this safe, high-quality meat that is delicious.

ANDORRANS

THE FIRST WRITTEN DOCUMENTATION OF people living in the valleys of Andorra was created by the Greek historian Polybius, who described a group known as the Andosinos. Later, the Basques probably moved through the valleys on their way to permanent settlements in the western Pyrenees. Evidence of the Basque imprint is reflected in the numerous towns and physical features bearing Basque names. The Roman influence on the area is felt in the nation's legal system and the Catalan language, and several Roman archaeological finds have surfaced recently. The Muslim Moors passed through the region on their way to more important destinations in France and left only limited evidence of their passing. There were no significant conversions to Islam made in the valleys of Andorra.

Spanish Catalonia's border forms all of the southern frontier and most of the western border of Andorra. The easiest access to Andorra has always been from the south via the Valira River valley. The bishops of Urgell, who have served as co-princes since 1278, have mostly been Catalan. The imprint of Catalonian culture on Andorra is highly visible in the nation's food and dress as well as in the Catalan language. In fact, Andorra is the only country in the world where Catalan is the official language of the state. Andorrans and Catalonians share a common descent, even though the present population of the country has incorporated migrations through the last fifty years that have brought people from many different nations. Andorran history and the Catalan language are taught at schools in order to favor integration.

POPULATION

One of the first population censuses of Andorra's residents was conducted in 1176. The results listed an estimated population of 2,300 individuals.

Opposite: **An elderly Andorran man.**

Over the next seven and a half centuries the population remained remarkably stable, with only a slight increase in number. Research completed in 1929 by a scholar from The Ohio State University listed a 1920 census that recorded 4,309 inhabitants. Over a period of 744 years Andorra's population had grown only by 2,009 individuals. Placed in perspective, these numbers reveal an average annual growth of fewer than three people a year.

Significant increases in population did not occur until after World War II. By 1960, the total population had increased to 8,392, and 15 years later the number had tripled to 25,000. Over the next 20 years the number would triple again, to reach 78,549 in 2005. Most of these increases were due to immigration, as foreign workers were attracted by the good wages supported by a booming economy.

With the influx of foreigners to Andorra, native Andorrans have become a minority in their own country.

The increasing number of foreigners turned the census figures upside down. Andorrans became a minority in their own country. In 1920 only 5 percent of the population was made up of foreign nationals. By 1987 that number had peaked at almost 80 percent of the population. Since then there has been a gradual decrease in the number of foreign residents, which now stands at approximately 60 percent of the population. In the most recent census Andorran citizens edged out Spanish nationals by slightly less than 1 percent to become the largest group in the country, although they still are not the majority.

Spaniards have always pre-dominated in the number of immigrants entering Andorra. Most are salaried workers, management executives, or small-business owners. The number of workers arriving from Portugal has increased dramatically, with men working mainly in construction and

The average age of the Andorran population is 36 years.

women taking positions in the hotel and restaurant sectors. The number of French immigrants has been steadily decreasing. The Spanish, Portuguese, and French account for almost 90 percent of foreign residents. Most of the remaining foreigners are retirees from European nations or workers from South America. British expatriates make up the largest sector of the retirement community, with significant numbers found in La Massana and Canillo.

The pattern of population settlement reflects the geography of the country. Almost the entire population is concentrated in towns linked to the major highways that follow the Y shape of Andorra's major river valleys. More than half the country's population is located in Andorra la Vella and its neighboring urban complex, Escaldes-Engordany. Encamp, Sant Julià de Lòria, and La Massana are also important urban centers although

Portuguese construction workers completing the roof on a local house.

they are much smaller. The vast majority of the mountainous terrain in Andorra is unpopulated or sparsely populated.

CITIZENSHIP

Attaining citizenship in Andorra is extremely difficult. This fact helps explain why Andorrans are a minority in their own country. Citizenship is guaranteed to all children whose parents are Andorran citizens. The process of gaining citizenship through naturalization can be difficult and generally takes a long period of time. Those foreigners who are eligible for citizenship are individuals who marry Andorrans and can prove that they have been permanent and continuous residents of the country for a minimum of three years. The children of these types of marriages are automatically full citizens. Other eligible immigrants are those who have established a permanent residency in the principality for at least 20 years. Children of foreign nationals who are born in Andorra can claim citizenship on their 18th birthday if they have lived permanently in the country since birth. Recent changes in the law have relaxed some of these rules. No Andorran citizen can claim dual citizenship with another nation.

REQUIREMENTS FOR PASSIVE RESIDENCY PERMITS

- own or lease a house or apartment
- pass a medical test regarding certain diseases
- provide proof of no criminal record
- present evidence of having a private health insurance plan
- spend at least 183 days in the country each year
- register and insure a vehicle in Andorra
- apply for an Andorran driver's license
- certify that the individual has an annual income of more than 30,000 euros, plus 10,000 euros for each dependent
- deposit 30,000 euros, plus 7,000 euros for each dependent, with the Government Finance Agency that is listed as an interest-free loan to the Andorran government and is refunded at the time the individual surrenders his or her residence

Opposite: **Children in Andorra are automatically granted citizenship if at least one of their parents is a citizen of the country.**

RESIDENCY PERMITS

To live in Andorra as a noncitizen, residents must file for one of two types of permits: a Work Residence Permit or a Passive Residence Permit. The Passive Residence Permit is designed to attract wealthy retirees who settle in Andorra to take advantage of its tax laws, banking secrecy, and high quality of life. The program is restricted to a quota of 500 individuals per year, and the permits are expensive. Most applicants for this type of permit originate in the United Kingdom, Germany, Belgium, the Netherlands, and Denmark. Very few people have settled in Andorra as passive residents.

When Andorra's economy expanded rapidly after World War II, the country recognized that it did not have enough native laborers to meet the needs of the increasing labor market. Residential work permits were created to allow foreign workers to apply for temporary residence. To qualify for work permits, individuals are required to prove that local businesses have guaranteed their employment. Local business managers are then required to arrange the issuance of the permits from the Ministry of Justice and Internal Affairs before the workers are allowed to enter the country.

ETHNIC INTERACTION

Ethnic friction is practically nonexistent in Andorra, and the country has avoided the type of terrorist acts that have been a problem for other European countries. No major ethnic groups are hostile toward other groups, and Andorrans treat all visitors in an open and friendly manner. Perhaps the basic explanation for ethnic harmony is that few cultural differences exist between Andorrans and most of their guest workers. Although Catalan is the official language, most residents are multilingual, with many speaking Spanish or French and a little English. Religious differences cause few problems, because the majority of the population is Roman Catholic. Hatred and revenge issues generated by wars and ethnic conflicts are nonexistent in Andorra, as compared to places like the Balkans and the former Soviet republics. Most nationalities mix comfortably with each other on a social basis, and different ethnic groups have not created their own isolated ghettos.

SOCIAL STRATIFICATION

Grinding poverty is not evident in Andorra, and both citizens and noncitizens live well above the poverty line. A clear difference, however, does exist between the social status of native Andorrans and guest workers. Andorrans own almost all of the privately owned land, businesses, and local industries. Most of this population is middle to upper class, and the types of residences they have reflect this economic success. Many native Andorrans live in spacious, expensive homes with small gardens and beautiful landscaping on the perimeter of the urban centers. If they do not own a private home, they rent luxury apartments with coveted private parking spaces. These apartment complexes are also located

on the edges of the cities, away from the constant traffic congestion. The middle- to upper-class residents are also conscious of international fashion trends and purchase well- known brands of designer clothing. Automobiles are status symbols, and many Andorrans own Mercedes, Audis, and BMWs.

Some foreign nationals, particularly the Spanish and the French, have secured salaried jobs in executive positions or government service that pay quite well. Others have become successful merchants in the duty-free shops or have purchased and manage restaurants, delis, and pastry shops that give them comfortable incomes. Still, the majority of the foreign nationals earn lower wages, engaging in the hard manual labor necessary for the society to function. These foreign laborers live in small efficiency apartments, drive economical compact cars or scooters or use public transportation, and wear clothing designed for work, not for making fashion statements. The salaries they earn are far in excess of what they would earn at home, and many send substantial amounts of currency (remittances) back to their countries of origin to help support their families. The foreign nationals generally appreciate the working conditions and wages available in Andorra, and many of them renew their work permits year after year.

Almost all of the inhabitants of Andorra live in narrow valleys that are surrounded by mountains.

LIFESTYLE

AN ACCOUNT OF ANDORRA WRITTEN MORE than a century ago described massive stone houses covered with slate roofs that provided no signs of change over the past few centuries. The people were described as cheerful, self-reliant, fearless, and poor. It was a reflection of a society in which change was barely noticeable. Then, over a period of a little more than a half century, change occurred at warp speed, morphing a largely pastoral society into a complex urban dynamo.

RURAL LIFE

Early settlement patterns in Andorra reflected those of much of Europe. Most individual farms were not scattered uniformly across the landscape, such as those on the Great Plains of the United States. Rather, farmers settled together in rural hamlets strung out along the river valleys. This pattern was shaped by three important controls. First, the population concentrations provided an element of defense as opposed to the vulnerability of an isolated farmstead. Second, the flat surfaces along the river plains were composed of the richest soils in the country. Finally, water was readily available for domestic needs, livestock, and irrigation. During the summers the land along the valleys was cultivated intensively, producing grains, hay, vegetables, and fruit. Later, tobacco became an important crop.

The second link in this largely subsistence-based rural economy was livestock. Each summer herds of sheep, goats, cattle, and mules were moved to the high pastures for several months. The meadow land was controlled by the parish governments under communal rules. While some of the family members remained in the valleys to cultivate their land, others followed the livestock into the mountains. There, life was hard. The herders lived part of the year in small, isolated stone houses without running water or electricity. Living conditions were primitive, yet a certain element of excitement accompanied the annual migration to the summer pastures.

Life centered on the family, and loyalty to family members was an unquestioned characteristic of Andorrans. The society was strongly patriarchal, and fathers had the first and last word. A father's authority was seldom questioned. Children were expected to contribute to the family workload early in their lives, and they were taught the necessity of developing a strong work ethic. The Catholic Church played a dominant role in almost all aspects of society, and participation in church activities was both expected and practiced.

Inheritance traditions had a stabilizing effect on population size over the centuries. Generally, the oldest son, the *hereu*, inherited three-quarters

Livestock herders use bordas, simple stone houses that are scattered across the alpine meadows, during the summer months when they followed their livestock into the mountains.

of the family estate, including the family home. Frequently, the other heirs gave their quarter of the land holdings to the oldest son in order to keep the entire farm in one piece for future generations. Because surplus farmland was not available and employment opportunities outside of the agricultural sector were almost nonexistent, many young adults emigrated to other European countries. A woman could inherit the land if there was no male heir. At one point there were more Andorrans living outside the country's borders than within its borders. The emigration of citizens was the main factor keeping Andorra's population from increasing for centuries.

Rural life today is almost a mirage. In 2005, a total of 138 people were employed in agriculture. The annual migration of livestock into the alpine meadows has been reduced to fewer than 5,000 animals each year. The only significant crop is tobacco, which will probably disappear within the next five years, when the tobacco subsidies are removed. The plots of land used to grow tobacco occupy some of the most valuable real estate in Andorra, frequently providing a rural environment in the midst of urban settings. The patches of green mixed among the chaos of unplanned urban development provide some of the visual treasures that attract tourists. The decisions about the type of land use allowed to develop on these limited agricultural lands will have a lasting impact on the future of Andorra.

THE URBAN SCENE

The transformation of Andorra from a rural society to an urban society is complete. While the family as a unit remains intact, the structure and function has changed dramatically. Farm life has been exchanged for commercial life, and economic activity now centers on family ownership

Life in Andorra is now centered on commercial activities.

Andorra has a very low crime rate and one police officer for every 220 inhabitants.

of retail shops, wholesale distribution centers, restaurants, car dealerships, and many other activities. While the eldest son is still likely to inherit the family business, there is now room for other children to participate as equal members in the business operations.

The dominant role of the father in the family is still apparent, but his unquestioned authority over family matters is eroding. Women are viewed as equals in Andorran society, where they hold high positions in both public and private sectors. More Andorran women attend universities than men, and women contribute to the national workforce in ever-increasing numbers.

The average number of children in a family has declined significantly, which is a common trend in societies experiencing a rural-to-urban change. Because women are now an important part of the workforce, much of the responsibility of raising children has shifted from the home to childcare centers and then to the schools. The time children spend with parents has been substantially reduced by the demands of workdays that often extend from early morning to late evening. The retail shops that dominate the employment sector are open every weekend and close for only four days each year. Some psychologists suggest that the insufficient development of relationships between parents and children is contributing to poorly adjusted youth who are lacking in social maturity. Such a trend is not surprising. Similar patterns can be easily observed in societies like the United States and western Europe where similar dysfunctional families have been formed during the urbanization process, with its focus on materialism.

A criticism frequently expressed in Andorra is that teenagers now view their homes as hotels. They sleep at home, eat there, and do their laundry there, but quality time spent with parents is minimal, as most teenagers prefer to spend their evenings hanging out with friends. Even with the declining interaction among family members, most children remain at home into their mid- to late twenties. Purchasing a house or even renting an apartment is a serious financial challenge for young Andorrans in a rapidly growing real estate market.

LIFE IN ANDORRA LA VELLA

Nowhere in Andorra is the pace of life more exiting than in its capital city, Andorra la Vella. It is the commercial, social, and political heart of this small nation. Traffic congestion and air pollution can be stifling, yet residents love their city. The ever cheerful traffic police, dressed in their colorful uniforms, guide traffic through the narrow streets with exaggerated arm motions and big smiles.

A walk through the Barri Antic (Old Town) at dusk reveals a slice of life with many different scenes. Old men sit on benches, leaning on canes, discussing the deterioration of youth as purple-haired, tattooed youngsters

The law allowing divorce in Andorra was not signed by one of the co-princes, the bishop of Urgell. However, divorce is legal because the French co-prince and the sindic general (speaker of parliament) signed the law.

Opposite: **The Parish of Ordino has many small villages and hamlets that attract many tourists who want a glimpse into Andorran traditional life.**

CASA DE LA VALL

No one building symbolizes the isolated mountain heritage of Andorra like the Casa de la Vall. The Busquets family originally built this impressive building as their family home in 1580. In 1702, the building was purchased by the Council of the Land and designated as the seat of parliament. Currently the building serves as both a museum and the active meeting place for the General Council. The chamber where parliament meets is impressive and intimate with photos of the two coprinces, the president of France and the bishop of Urgell, quietly observing the conduct of the central government. The spacious kitchen, with its antique utensils, has been perfectly preserved and displays a clear image of life in the 16th century. Other rooms contain a criminal court, a small jail, and a salon with beautiful frescoes representing the Passion of Christ.

with iPods or cell phones attached to their ears pass by. Upwardly mobile, young career women sit in cafés sipping lattes. A small gathering of professional men can be observed in popular bars, having a drink while snacking on plates of cheese and meat and discussing politics and business. Many smoke, as the long history of growing tobacco has left a deep imprint on the social habits of Andorrans.

The evidence of construction is everywhere. Cranes cast a silhouette across the skyline. Backhoes rip at the rock surface in an attempt to clear a flat spot for yet another building. Modern architecture mixes with traditional building styles. Nowhere is this difference more apparent than in the building that houses the offices of the national government and the Casa de la Vall, the seat of parliament. The former is a stylish concrete and glass construction, while the latter is a 16th-century stone building that gives the appearance of a palace-fortress.

TRADITIONAL VILLAGES

Villages such as Pal, Sispony, La Cortinada, Segudet, and Ordino reflect a slower pace of life in more traditional settings. Historical evidence of the past is represented by restored iron forges, sawmills, Romanesque churches, and homes

Students board a bus to school. Parents are able to choose from three types of schools to send their children.

that were owned by some of Andorra's leading families. Tourists are attracted by opportunities to stroll through history in quiet settings and quaint, small-town environments. Even new homes reflect the traditional mountain style of architecture as a result of parish regulations that require a certain percentage of building fronts to be covered with natural stone.

EDUCATION

The literacy rate in Andorra is 100 percent, as Andorrans place a high value on education. Children are required to attend school until they reach the age of 16, but almost all students complete high school. The education system is somewhat unique in that parents can send their children to one of three types of schools. At the primary and secondary levels, school attendance is divided almost equally, with one-third of the students attending Andorran, Spanish, and French schools, respectively. The presence of the French and Spanish schools is a historic carryover from the time when Andorra requested the help of its neighbors in order to provide its youth with a modern education.

The schools are built and maintained by Andorran authorities, but the teachers in the French and Spanish schools are paid by their respective governments. The Spanish and Andorran schools follow the Spanish curriculum, while the French schools adhere to the French curriculum. The Andorran school system has developed a unique curriculum and is now incorporating the example of the Finnish school system. All three systems place a great emphasis on language education, with required courses in Catalan, Spanish, and French. Recently, English has also been introduced into the curriculum.

The University of Andorra was established in 1997, but the small population of available students restricts the number of academic disciplines the university can offer. The university, for example, offers a standard program in computer science, a nursing school, and a Masters of Business Administration program, which is offered at night for working individuals. Seventy percent of Andorran university students are enrolled in universities in Spain and France, particularly in Barcelona and Toulouse.

HEALTH CARE

Andorrans have the longest life expectancy in the world, at 83.51 years. While genetics undoubtedly contribute to a long life, so does diet and exercise. The general population descended from sturdy mountain people who ate a balanced diet and got plenty of exercise from raising their crops and livestock. Today's Andorrans follow the same dietary habits of their ancestors, work long hours, and spend much of their leisure time hiking and skiing.

Medical care is guaranteed to all citizens and foreigners holding legal work permits. The capital city has a modern general hospital and a number of government clinics and private medical centers. Indeed, all Andorran communities provide access to family medical service. A social security tax of 18 percent of each employee's salary funds the health care system. Employees pay 5 percent, while employers contribute 13 percent. Ten percent of the money raised from this tax is set aside for health care, and 8 percent is reserved to pay old-age benefits.

RELIGION

THE PEOPLE OF ANDORRA HAD ACCEPTED Christianity by the 6th century, when the first bishop of Urgell was appointed. The continuing influence of the diocese of Urgell ensured that over the next several centuries, more than 90 percent of Andorrans would be Roman Catholics. In 1278 the bishop of Urgell became one of the two co-princes who served as an equal head of state with the count of Foix. The clergy appointed to the parish churches in Andorra followed the policies of the bishop of Urgell and maintained strict supervision over their parishioners. Church members were expected to attend services regularly and were encouraged to tithe from their personal wealth. Questions regarding church policy and doctrines were not entertained by the priests, and few people strayed from the religious teachings of the Roman Catholic Church.

Left: **The wood-and-gold-carved altar at Sant Martí de la Cortinada church.**

Opposite: **The Church Benaurats in Andorra la Vella.**

The sacraments, including baptism, first communion, confirmation, marriage, and last rights, were bestowed on landmark days in the lives of the believers. The church was the depository for family records and held the responsibility for registering births, marriages, and deaths. The church was also the center of social activity. Sunday masses provided a respite from the long hours of work on the farms and brought neighbors together for a day of rest and reflection. After services the men discussed farm matters and parish politics, the women gathered on the church porches to talk about their families, and the children played in the churchyards.

During the 19th and 20th centuries political events in neighboring France and Spain began to erode the power of the clergy. Church attendance began to decline, and some citizens began to push for schools that were secular rather than completely controlled by the Catholic Church. The choice to eat meat on Fridays was accepted, and tithing was abandoned by most families. After 1950, rapid urbanization continued to alter the role of the church in Andorran society.

THE NEW AGE

The Roman Catholic Church was the official church of Andorra until the 1993 constitution liberalized religious freedom. Article 11 of the constitution guarantees "the freedom of ideas, religion and cult, and no one is bound to state or disclose his or her ideology, religion or beliefs." While the constitution no longer designates the Roman Catholic Church as the official state religion, it does acknowledge that the Church has a special relationship with the country of Andorra. "The Constitution guarantees the Roman Catholic Church free and public exercise of its activities and the preservation of the relations of special cooperation with the State in accordance with the Andorran tradition."

This special relationship is reflected in many ways. Some public ceremonies may be accompanied by a Catholic mass. Instruction on the Catholic faith is available in public schools if parents select that option. The religion classes are held outside regular school hours, but the government pays the religion teachers. Almost 25 percent of primary students attend these classes, but only 1 percent of secondary students enroll in these special educational opportunities. The parish priests are also paid from government revenues.

The role of the Catholic Church in shaping social policy is also reflected in the constitution, which defends life in all its phases and prohibits capital punishment. Other social positions supported by the Church are not rigidly followed by many Andorrans. It is now legal to be married in a civil ceremony, acquire a divorce, and practice birth control. Many Andorrans live together before getting married, in opposition to Church policy.

Ninety percent of Andorrans still declare themselves to be Roman Catholics. A recent opinion poll conducted by the Institute of Andorran Studies revealed that 52 percent of those polled considered themselves as very religious people. On the other hand, almost half of the Catholic population is not active in church life. This pattern of nonparticipation is more common in the urbanized areas, where many Andorrans work in the duty-free shops on Sundays. Church participation in the more rural parishes, such as Ordino and Sant Julià de Lòria, is generally higher. Religious participation is also age specific, with older members remaining active, while many of the nation's youth are abandoning regular church attendance.

Sant Martí de la Cortinada is one of Andorra's most famous Romanesque churches.

ROMANESQUE CHURCHES

The true treasures of Andorran history are the thirty Romanesque churches built between the 9th and 13th centuries. They were the early centers of spiritual and community life for the pious mountain people of Andorra. The churches are, for the most part, well-preserved and maintained. Originally constructed along the old dirt roads and trails, many served as sentinels looking out over the valleys. The bell towers served not only to call the faithful to services but also as defensive positions that allowed for the observation of intruders entering the parishes.

The fact that most of these churches have survived a thousand years of history is a testimony to their sturdy construction from rock readily

This is one of many frescoes that was discovered at the church of Sant Martí de la Cortinada.

available at the sites. The lack of war within the nation's boundaries also helped prevent the destruction of these uniquely simple yet impressive edifices. The interiors of some of the churches contain stunning religious frescoes and elaborate wood-carved altars.

Sant Martí de la Cortinada, near Ordino, is one of the most beloved of all the Romanesque churches. The main church was constructed during the 12th century, but it underwent major additions and renovations in the 17th and 18th centuries. During these renovations, the removal of plaster on some of the interior walls revealed beautiful frescoes of St. Martin, the bishop of Tours, and a mythological wolflike animal with a forked tongue. Four separate altars from the 18th century represent a style known as Andorran Baroque. Two paintings on the main altar depict the Nativity and the Adoration of the Kings.

THE SANCTUARIES

Andorra has two noted sanctuaries, both of which are important sites for religious pilgrimages. The Sanctuary of Meritxell, dedicated to Our Lady of Meritxell, the patron saint of Andorra, is the most important religious site in Andorra. On September 8 each year great numbers of pilgrims from across Andorra, as well as from Spain and France, gather at the site for a day-long ceremony. The event is a national holiday and one of only four days during the year when all businesses must remain closed.

In 1658, a new building replaced the original Romanesque structure at the site. Fire destroyed the church in 1972, along with its priceless Gothic-style wood carving dedicated to Our Lady of Meritxell. The loss of the sanctuary and the carving caused great anguish for the Andorran people. A large new sanctuary, designed by the famous Catalan architect Ricardo Bofill, was completed in 1976. The new sanctuary is constructed from traditional stone and black slate but reflects a modern architectural design. In 1994, a portion of the old sanctuary was restored to house an exhibit called Meritxell Memory. The exhibit is a collection of photos, texts, and objects that help preserve the collective memory of the citizens of Andorra.

The Sanctuary of the Virgin of Canòlich is located high on a mountainside in the parish of Sant Julià de Lòria. In a duplication of history the old Romanesque structure also burned to the ground. However, the ancient

A sanctuary that honors the Virgin of Canólich.

altarpiece dedicated to the Virgin Mary survived the fire. A simple new structure was constructed between 1973 and 1979. Each year, on the last Saturday in May, hundreds of pilgrims arrive at the sanctuary to participate in one of the most popular religious festivals in the country.

MINORITY RELIGIOUS GROUPS

Only a small number of other religious organizations exist in the largely Roman Catholic Andorra. Most of the members of these groups belong to such denominations as the Anglican Church, Jehovah's Witnesses, or the Church of Jesus Christ of Latter-day Saints (Mormons). There is also a small Muslim community of approximately 500 individuals who are mostly Moroccans living in Andorra on Work Residency Permits. There are a few Hindus and Buddhists and a small Jewish community with approximately 100 members.

All of the minority religious groups practice their faith without discrimination. Missionaries for both the Mormons and the Jehovah's Witnesses go door-to-door in an attempt to recruit new members, without any restrictions. The Jewish community recently opened a synagogue and cultural center and is well integrated into Andorran society. The Islamic Cultural Center provides Arabic lessons for young people who are mostly of North African descent. The Catholic Church of La Massana has granted the use of its sanctuary twice a month for the Anglican parishioners who represent several hundred retired British citizens living in Andorra. Recently, the government of Andorra sponsored a meeting dedicated to the continued improvement of the respect for religious freedom. The bishop of Urgell and co-prince Joan Enric Vives i Sicilía presided over the meeting, which included Catholics, Protestants, Jews, Muslims, Buddhists, and Hindus.

THE STORY OF THE VIRGIN OF MERITXELL

The Gothic-style wood carving of an image of the Virgin of Meritxell dated to the 12th or 13th century. The story says that a shepherd or small group of people found the statue surrounded by flowers that were blooming out of season on a snowy hillside. The statue was moved to the nearest hamlet for protection but disappeared during the night. The next day the statue was found at the original site of discovery. This routine occurred three times, and finally the people decided that this was a sign from God to build a church at that specific location. The new sanctuary (*below*) contains a copy of the original statue of the Virgin of Meritxell.

LIGATORI SEGUIR TOT
ORMES DE SEGURETA

PROHIBIT EL PAS
A TOTA PERSONA
ALIENA A L'OBRA

LANGUAGE

ANDORRA IS TRULY A MULTILINGUAL society. The number of languages spoken there is a reflection of the diversity of people who live in Andorra or visit the country as tourists. While Catalan is the official language, Spanish, French, Portuguese, and English are also commonly heard on the streets. Other minority languages include Arabic, German, Italian, and Dutch.

The 1993 constitution made Catalan the official language of the state. It is a beautiful language of which Andorrans are very proud and also committed to maintaining. Catalan is one of the Romance languages. It developed between the 8th and 10th centuries. The language began to be used in written texts during the 12th century and has gone through periods of prominence and decline, based on political issues and control. The first known texts written in the Catalan language come from the village of Organyà, situated very close to the Andorran-Spanish border. The Spanish cities of Barcelona and Valencia were early centers of Catalan usage, and prominent writers and poets distinguished themselves in the language during the 13th and 14th centuries. The language spread from the Pyrenees Mountains in the High Middle Ages southward, following the reconquest of the area from the Moors. It also became the language of choice of southeastern France, of the Balearic Islands, and of the city of Alghero, on Sardinia's northeastern coast.

In the early 1700s, King Philip V of Spain abolished the governmental institutions of Catalonia and introduced Spanish laws. In some instances the use of Catalan was prohibited or seriously repressed. The intellectual use of Catalan largely disappeared, and the language became most commonly used in private conversations or in the safety of individual homes.

A cultural rebirth of the use of Catalan, known as the Renaixença (Renaissance), blossomed during the second half of the 19th century,

Opposite: **A warning sign in Catalan.**

Opposite: **The national office building of the Government of Andorra houses the offices of the prime minister and most of his cabinet ministers. All officials must be proficient in Catalan.**

with poetry contests and the rise of noted writers who used Catalan. In the early 1900s, standardized spelling rules, a dictionary, and rules of grammar were published. By the 1930s, Catalan had been restored as the official language of Catalonia. However, the outbreak of the Spanish Civil War, in 1936, and the establishment of the fascist dictatorship of Francisco Franco resulted in the prohibition of the use of Catalan in Spain.

Since 1975, the use of Catalan has again been restored across the traditionally Catalan-speaking areas of Spain. The widespread usage of the Catalan language now covers approximately 26,481 square miles (68,000 square km), with 13.5 million speakers. Recent estimates suggest that 9 to 10 million individuals in this group can speak Catalan, while a total of 11 million can understand the language. In Spain, Catalan is the co-official language in Catalonia, Valencia, and the Balearic Islands. Andorra is the only country in the world where Catalan is, and has always remained, the single official language. In 1993, when Andorra was given full membership in the United Nations, Prime Minister Oscar Ribas Reig became the first diplomat to address the United Nations General Assembly in Catalan.

LAW OF OFFICIAL LANGUAGE USE PLANNING

The citizens of Andorra are serious about protecting the rich heritage and traditions of the Catalan language. In 1999, the General Council passed and the co-princes signed the Law of Official Language Use Planning. The law contains 41 articles designed to guarantee the official use of Catalan.

The central government and local parish administrations must use Catalan in conducting business. All government publications are required to be printed in Catalan. Catalan must be used in schools, the mass media, sports, and cultural activities. It is the language of the entire judicial system, and all courts require that attorneys and judges be fluent in Catalan. All traffic signs, advertising media, and names of shops must be printed in Catalan. Hotels, bars, and restaurants must write their menus, price lists, service lists, and public information in Catalan. This material may also be printed in other languages, but always as secondary information. Any employee who wishes to work in public administration (national or local government) is required to pass an oral and written proficiency test in Catalan.

LANGUAGE AND EDUCATION

The Andorran education system is a multi-lingual one in which language training is the centerpiece of the curriculum. There are three different systems parents can select for their children: the Andorran schools, the French schools, and the Spanish schools. Currently, approximately one-third of students attend each of the systems, respectively.

In the Andorran schools, Catalan is taught at every grade level, from pre-school through high school. French is also taught in pre-school, while Spanish and English

are introduced in primary school. When students enter high school, they begin a rigorous schedule that requires 12 hours of language training every week—three hours each for Catalan, Spanish, French, and English.

In the French schools French is used as the language of instruction throughout the program. Catalan is taught as a language course by Catalan-speaking teachers from pre-school through high school. When students enter high school, they are allowed to choose either Spanish or English as a third language for two years. In the last two years of high school French, Catalan, Spanish, and English are required courses for three hours each week. In the past more than half of Andorran students were enrolled in the French schools, but enrollment has been steadily declining.

The Spanish schools use both Spanish and Catalan as languages of instruction. If Spanish is the medium of instruction, Catalan is offered as a required language class, and if Catalan is the medium of instruction, Spanish is the required language class. This pattern exists from pre-school through high school. During primary school, English and French are introduced, but students choose one of them. When they reach high school, students will normally elect to continue to study French or English, but not both languages.

MINORITY LANGUAGES

Almost 90 percent of all foreign nationals living in Andorra are citizens of Spain, Portugal, or France. In addition, the bulk of tourists visiting Andorra arrive from Spain or France. As a result, Spanish, French, and Portuguese are the languages most commonly spoken in Andorra. In fact, not enough foreigners make the effort to learn Catalan because it is a difficult language to learn, and almost everyone in the country speaks some Spanish, French, or English.

There is little doubt, and statistics prove it, that Spanish has already become the social language of Andorra. It is the native tongue of at least one-third of the population and the majority of the tourists. Almost all of the clerks in the duty-free shops as well as workers in hotels, bars, restaurants, and ski resorts know some conversational Spanish.

The use of French as a means of communication has been steadily declining. French schools no longer dominate Andorra's educational system, and the number of Andorran students who attend French universities has decreased noticeably. French is still spoken extensively along the eastern border, in the city of El Pas de la Casa, and in the ski resorts where French ski enthusiasts arrive in large buses as a part of group travel packages.

The sounds of the Portuguese language are common at construction sites, at jobs that emphasize hard physical labor, and among Portuguese workers in hotels and restaurants. Few Andorrans speak Portuguese, but significant numbers can understand the language. While Portuguese

Andorra has almost twice as many cellular telephones as standard landline phones.

DAYS OF THE WEEK

A unique aspect of the Catalan language is that every day of the week begins with the letter D.

Monday	*Dilluns*
Tuesday	*Dimarts*
Wednesday	*Dimecres*
Thursday	*Dijous*
Friday	*Divendres*
Saturday	*Dissabte*
Sunday	*Diumenge*

workers communicate with each other in Portuguese, most can also speak and understand some Spanish, and some are learning Catalan.

Near La Massana and Canillo, English is spoken by a core group of British retirees who live in Andorra on Passive Resident Permits. While few older Andorrans speak English, most schoolchildren and teenagers speak and understand some English. Their exposure to English in the schools as well as through movies, television, video games, and music contributes to a growing literacy in English for young Andorrans.

MASS MEDIA

Historically, Andorra's proximity to both Spain and France has meant easy access to television and radio broadcasts from its neighbors. One exception was the development of a powerful domestic radio station that went on the air in 1939. Broadcasting with 60,000 watts of power, Radio Andorra could be heard across much of western Europe.

All types of modern media are now available in Andorra. Andorra la Vella is the site of the first Andorran television station, which started in 1997 and broadcasts all its programs in Catalan. Twenty FM radio stations provide music, news, and special programming to loyal listeners. Telephone services are available through both landlines and mobile cellular systems operated by the Andorran Telecommunications Service. Internet connections are easily available at both business locations and in private homes, while tourists have easy access to Internet cafés in most parts of the country. The country has four popular daily newspapers: *El Periòdic*, *Diari d'Andorra*, *Bon Dia*, and *Més*, which publish daily in Catalan. Free postal service within the country as well as regular international postal services are provided, under concession, by the French and Spanish postal systems.

LANGUAGES OF ANDORRA: WORDS AND PHRASES

English	Catalan	Spanish	French
Hello	Hola	Hola	Bonjour
Good-bye	Adéu	Adios	Au revoir
Thank you	Gràcies	Gracias	Merci
Rabbit	Cunill	Conejo	Lapin
Sheep	Ovella	Oveja	Mouton
Chicken	Gall	Gallo	Poulet
Red	Vermell	Rojo	Rouge
Green	Vert	Verde	Vert
Black	Negre	Negro	Noir
Blue	Blau	Azul	Bleu
River	Riu	Rio	Rivière
Lake	Llac	Lago	Lac
Mountain	Montanya	Montaña	Montagne

Phrases:			
I don't understand.	No ho entenc.	No entiendo.	Je ne comprends pas.
Do you speak English?	Parles anglès?	Habla inglés?	Parlez-vous anglais?
Excuse me.	Dispensi/Perdoni.	Disculpe/Perdoni.	Excusez-moi.

NONVERBAL COMMUNICATIONS

Many standard forms of nonverbal communications are common in Andorra. A handshake is the customary form of greeting, although relatives and close friends may exchange a hug or a kiss on the cheek. A shrug of the shoulders usually signifies "I do not know" or "I do not care." A rolling of the eyes implies a lack of belief or a suggestion that the speaker is exaggerating. If invited for dinner, guests may provide a nonverbal thank you by presenting the hostess with flowers and the host with a bottle of wine. It would be inconsiderate, however, to present roses to the hostess, because roses imply a romantic interest. The victory sign and thumbs-up are used frequently.

ARTS

ANY DISCUSSION OF THE ROLE of the arts in Andorra requires an understanding of the type of society that existed throughout most of the country's formal political existence dating back to 1278. It has always been a small nation with a population that seldom exceeded 5,000 inhabitants. Andorra had no great academic centers or universities to foster intellectual thought or the creative arts. Communication with the outside world was infrequent, and the exchange of ideas was limited to what little information penetrated the country's frontiers via a narrow river valley connecting to Spain and a high mountain pass connecting to France. The Roman Catholic Church offered mostly conservative ideological doctrines and discouraged intellectual curiosity.

Early artistic expression was limited primarily to the rural architecture of the family home, which displayed a rugged mountain style. Houses were large, multistory structures that utilized natural stone for the outside walls, local slate for roof coverings, and heavy wooden beams, doors, and window shutters. Furniture was crafted by local artisans and frequently included primitive carvings to convey individuality. In the high meadows, livestock herders built beautiful but simple stone houses, frequently without the use of mortar. Their thick circular or rectangular stone walls provided basic protection for the herders during the summer months.

The Romanesque style of architecture had a significant impact on the small stone churches of Andorra and a few simple bridges. Andorran

Above: **The doorway of a Romanesque church in Andorra.**

Opposite: **The dancing statue of Andorra la Vella on the grounds of the parliament building. The statue celebrates 100 years of reform.**

Romanesque art is appreciated internationally, as evidenced by some high-quality art pieces found in museums as far away as Boston, Massachusetts. Examples of both Baroque and Gothic art forms were present in the early churches, and some are preserved today. Music was limited to religious hymns and chants or the traditional compositions that accompanied local festivals and folkloric dances. Original Andorran literature did not appear until the 19th century.

The 20th century saw a broad awakening in the arts throughout the country. Both the central government and the local parish administrations began to provide financial support for the promotion and advancement of multiple expressions of artistic creativity. The arts thrive today in Andorra at a level unusual for a nation of its size.

Tourists on the Roman bridge of La Margineda. Roman architecture can be found throughout Andorra.

ARCHITECTURE

The thirty Romanesque churches of Andorra are sources of great pride to its citizens. Frequently, they are small structures perched on high promontories overlooking river valleys, such as the Church of Sant Cristòfol d'Anyós. The churches are characterized by simplicity and a lack of architectural clutter on their exteriors. The dominant exterior feature is almost always the square or cylindrical Lombard-style bell tower. Several of the churches also have attached porches that were used for both social and religious functions.

The interiors range from simple to complex and display several artistic styles. Eleven churches retain frescoes in a variety of stages of preservation. The Master of Santa Coloma and the Master of La Cortinada, who were influenced by the great artists of that period, such as Taull, Pedret, and Urgell, painted the most impressive frescoes. At the Church of Sant Joan de Caselles, Romanesque-style stucco sculptures of the Virgin Mary and of Christ in His Majesty adorn the interior.

Romanesque architecture is also represented by the classically beautiful rural bridges that still exist in Andorra. The best example of the original stone bridges that date to the 9th century is the bridge of La Margineda. This exquisitely preserved thousand-year-old bridge spans the Valira River between Sant Julià de Lòria and Andorra la Vella. Narrow but elegant, the bridge stretches for 108 feet (33 m) across the river and has weathered countless floods through the centuries.

The influence of modern architectural design is becoming apparent in many Andorran towns. Two of the most recognized buildings that reflect modern styles are the central government building in Andorra la Vella and the Caldea spa complex in Escaldes. The government building is a concrete and glass structure with simple lines that provides a functional office setting. The Caldea complex is a stunning steel and blue glass structure that mimics the mountain peaks of the Pyrenees. Recently the minister of culture has started a program to bring to the country architects of world fame to work on public buildings. Los Angeles-based architect

The Caldea spa complex is one of Andorra's most recognizable and renown modern structures.

Frank Gehry has been hired to work on the new National Archives building in La Massana, and the search is on for the architect who will design a new national museum on government land in Santa Coloma.

LITERATURE

Anton Fiter i Rossell, an attorney born in Ordino, was the first writer of note from Andorra. In 1748, he published the Manual Digest, a compilation of Andorra's history, customs, traditional laws, and folk sayings. This important work is used for historical research. Later, Father Antoni Puig, a priest born in Encamp, completed a second significant historical publication, titled *Politar Andorrà*.

Currently, several Andorran writers have earned respect for their contributions to writing. Antoni Morell is a respected writer and president of the Andorran Writer's Association. Ricard Fiter i Vilajoana is a well-known author, attorney, and representative of Andorra to the Council of Europe. Ramon Villeró is an award-winning author who writes novels and does freelance writing. Michèle Gazier, who was born in Andorra but currently is living in France, has earned an excellent reputation as an author and literary critic. Joan Peruga has written a number of popular novels. The current spokesman of the government, Minister of Culture, and former Minister of Foreign Affairs Juli Minoves Triquell holds the Fiter i Rossell Prize for his novel *Segles de Memória*, and has published several works of fiction. Josep Enrich Dallerès is a noted poet. The National Library and National Archives were founded in 1930

Juli Minoves Triquell, is not only an established writer, he is also the former foreign affairs minister of Andorra.

and 1975, respectively, to house a rapidly growing body of literature and important documents.

MUSIC AND THEATER

Traditional folk music has always played an important role in local and national festivals, especially to accompany such dances as the *sardana* and *marratxa*. One of the most important songs penned in Andorran is its national anthem. It was officially adopted on September 8, 1914, the date of the national holiday that honors the patron saint of Andorra, Our Lady of Meritxell. The music was composed by Father Enric Marfany Bons, and the lyrics were written by Joan Benlloch i Vivò, bishop of Urgell and coprince of Andorra from 1906 to 1919.

Andorra has recently gained an international reputation for the development of its music programs. The National Auditorium in Ordino hosts an extended music season organized by the Ministry of Culture. International performers who have graced the building's performance hall include Yehudi Menuhin, Barbara Hendricks, José Carreras, Narciso Yepes, and the International Ballet of Cristina Hoyos.

ALBERT SALVADÓ

Today, Albert Salvadó is Andorra's most popular and best-selling author. He has written children's books, essays, and novels. The popularity of his books stems from his unique ability to weave reality, fiction, and mystery into his writing. His literary skill has been recognized with several awards, including the Second Néstor Luján Prize for the Historical Novel, the Fiter i Rossell Prize of the Circle of Arts and Letters, the First Planeta "Sèrie Negra" Prize, and the Carlemany Prize. Some of his best-known works are *The Master of Cheops, Attila's Ring, Death and the Man from Marseilles*, and *Hannibal's Eyes*.

This wall mural in Ordino celebrates the importance of classical music in Andorran society.

Andorra la Vella hosts the Season of Music and Dance from November to May each year, attracting many fine musicians and dancers, including the well-known pianists Evgeny Kissin and Ainhoa Arteta. In Sant Julià de Lòria, opera megastar Montserrat Caballé hosts the Montserrat Caballé International Singing Competition. Each July, jazz fans congregate in Escaldes-Engordany for the International Jazz Festival. This event historically has attracted some of the best jazz musicians in the world, including Miles Davis, B. B. King, and Fats Domino.

Andorra has produced two classical musicians of international fame. The Claret brothers were born in Ordino in 1951. Lluís Claret is a renowned cellist and winner of several international competitions. He is a founding member of the Trio de Barcelona and has been an invited soloist at prestigious orchestras across Europe. Gerard Claret is an internationally acclaimed violin soloist and teacher. In 1993, he was appointed concert conductor of the National Chamber Orchestra of Andorra (ONCA) and continues to serve as the director of the Narciso Yepes International Festival in Ordino. The National Chamber Orchestra frequently performs with the National Young Singers Choir of Andorra, an all-boy choir that is rapidly gaining recognition in Europe under the leadership of the talented Catherine Métayer. Recently the ONCA has been upgraded to the National Classical Orchestra of Andorra and performs with more than 55 musicians with Italian conductor Marzio Conti. An Andorran symphony composed by Maestro Sergio Rendine was recently produced to great acclaim.

Andorra entered the Eurovision Song Contest for the first time in 2004, with the first song performed in Catalan in the 50-year history of the contest. During the 2007 competition a local three-member band named Anonymous nearly reached the finals with its original song *Salvem el Món* (*Let's Save the World*).

During the theater season, sponsored jointly by Andorra la Vella and Sant Julià de Lòria, many distinguished actors have performed to appreciative audiences. José María Pou, star of movies, television, and theater, as well as a New York Times Critic's Choice, is one of the favorite performers. Paco Morán and Joan Pera, two of Spain's most popular actors, have also participated in theater productions in Andorra. In 2007, the government of Andorra created the National Theater of Andorra (ENA, or Escena Nacional d'Andorra), chaired by the minister of culture. Its first production was *A Streetcar Named Desire*, by the American playwright Tennessee Williams. The National Theater will also produce works of cinematography.

SCULPTURE

Josep Viladomat, a Spanish-born sculptor, fled Spain after the Spanish Civil War and settled in the parish of Escaldes. He was quickly adopted by the Andorran people, who recognized his creative talent. Working primarily with stone, he was an active artist whose works can be seen in galleries around the world. When he died, in 1989, the Viladomat Museum was created to honor his work, with displays of 250 sculptures.

In 1991, the people of Andorra initiated a new program to support modern sculpture. They hired more than a dozen internationally famous sculptors to create pieces that are now featured in select locations around the country. Two of the favorite exhibits are Denis Oppenheim's *Storm in a Teacup* and Paul van Hoeydonks's *Robot in Suspension*. Hoeydonk gained international attention when his sculpture *Fallen Astronaut* was placed on the moon during the Apollo 15 mission.

MUSEUMS AND MONUMENTS

The Andorran Cultural Heritage Museums and Monuments Department manages five national museums and two national monuments. Two of the five national museums are houses that preserve the traditional way of life in rural Andorra. One of the most influential families in La Massana parish lived in the Casa Rull in Sispony. Despite the family's influence, life was not easy; the furnishings reflect a life of economic struggle, not one of luxury. Casa Areny Plandolit, in Ordino, was a home designed and furnished for one of the aristocratic families of Andorra. The home was one of many owned by a family with financial interests in livestock, iron mines, and forges. Originally built in 1633, the house had one of the finest personal libraries in Europe, an elaborate set of china service (a gift from Austrian royalty), and its own personal chapel. The house was the first in the country to have running water, in the late 1800s, and electricity, in 1929.

Paul van Hoeydonk's sculpture, *Robot in Suspension*, is on permanent diplay in Andorra.

The remaining three national museums include the National Automobile Museum, which has a collection of approximately 100 antique cars and

The personal chapel of the Arney-Plandolit home that was authorized by the Catholic Church.

50 motorcycles. The Andorran Postal Museum has an incredible collection of Andorran stamps issued since 1928 by the French and Spanish postal services, which operates under contract. Current Andorran stamps are valued in euros and are only used for letters going outside the country, since internal mail is delivered free of charge. The Rossell Forge may be the most interesting museum in the country. The facility depicts the production of iron ingots precisely as it was when the forge was open, from 1845 to 1876. A skilled professional trained in the techniques used to produce the ingots illustrates the production process using a gigantic iron hammer powered by the same waterwheel employed a century and a half in the past.

The two national monuments are centerpiece selections that represent the church and the state. The Sanctuary of Meritxell is the spiritual center of Andorra's largely Roman Catholic population. Casa de la Vall is the active seat of government for the secular state. Parliament has met in this building since 1702, and the original kitchen is still intact. Construction was recently initiated for a new building to house the parliament.

The Pin Museum in Ansalonga contains 75,000 pins, which are classified into 110 different categories. It is the largest pin collection in the world and is listed in the Guinness Book of World Records.

LEISURE

THE MAJORITY OF ANDORRANS ARE urban dwellers and, though their bodies may be in the cities, their hearts and souls are in the mountains. Andorrans often grasp the opportunity to escape the city and engage in whatever physical activity is appropriate for the season in the sparsely populated rural areas. These hardy mountain people hike along old smuggling trails while enjoying nature. Andorrans are generally in excellent physical condition because of their active participation in both winter and summer recreational activities. Obesity is rare in Andorra, and healthy exercise routines have contributed to the longest life expectancy in the world.

Every day of the year, cities offer a wide range of leisure activities, primarily aimed toward the tourists who visit the country. Andorrans are committed to earning a living during the workweek and labor long hours in the duty-free shops, restaurants, and hotels. On the weekends they may participate in shopping themselves. They are a wealthy society that can afford to purchase internationally famous brands of clothing, jewelry, and electronics. After shopping, they may stroll through Andorra la Vella's Barri Antic (Old Town) while the last rays of the sun cast a golden glow over the mountains that surround the city. As they walk slowly past the Church of Saint Steven on quaint cobblestone streets, they can watch the central city's entertainment district come to life around the old public square.

WINTER ACTIVITIES

Nothing will start the flow of adrenaline in an Andorran's veins faster than the sight of the season's first snow. From November to March practically the entire population of the nation engages in skiing. During the season, skiing dominates almost every conversation, pushing politics,

Opposite: **Children learn to ski in Soldeu. Skiing is one of Andorran's favorite pasttimes.**

The Ice Palace of Andorra (Palau de Gel d'Andorra) in Canillo features an Olympic-size ice-skating rink.

105

economic issues, and gossip into the background. Children as young as 3 years of age attend ski lessons and, by the time they are teenagers, they are more comfortable in a pair of ski boots than a pair of shoes. Skiing is a love affair that continues into old age, with skiers in their 70s still hitting the slopes.

The introduction of skiing to Andorra came about through an unlikely event. A French postman who delivered the mail from France to Soldeu used snowshoes to help traverse the deep snows near El Pas de la Casa. While picking up a mail delivery in the French village of Porta, he observed the villagers moving about effortlessly on two long pieces of wood. When a particularly heavy snow occurred, he strapped on a pair of skis himself and headed for his delivery route in Andorra. This event changed Andorra dramatically as the Andorrans quickly adopted this new method of moving over snow. Today Andorra has the best skiing in the Pyrenees, and its citizens are among the most passionate ski enthusiasts in the world.

Hiking through Andorra's mountains is a wonderful way to experience the beauty of Andorra.

SUMMER ACTIVITIES

During the summer Andorrans trade their ski boots for hiking boots and head for the mountain trails. Hiking paths are located in every corner of the country, and trekking into the mountains to camp is a family tradition. There are more than 30 major, well-marked hiking paths.

Families or individuals can either pitch tents or stay in one of 26 stone camp houses provided free of charge by the government. Camping is a communal experience starting with pitching the tent. Everyone has a task to perform. Firewood must be gathered for the cooking fire. A few fresh trout must be caught in the nearby mountain stream or lake. A successful hunt for wild mushrooms, wild celery, and fresh dandelion greens will add some delicacies to meals. Early in the morning, just as the first rays of the sun sneak over the high mountain peaks, the smell of fresh-brewed coffee fills the air, and soon after the family indulges in slabs of smoked bacon and freshly cooked eggs. A weekend in the mountains allows families some quiet time together, away from the traffic congestion, air pollution, and noise so common in the valleys below.

David Ramon, an Andorran sailor, won one of eleven Olympic Solidarity Scholarships for training in sailing in 2000, even though Andorra is landlocked and has only small lakes not suited for sailing.

SPORTS

It is no surprise that the first organized sporting activity in Andorra was skiing. The Ski Andorra Club was organized in 1932. All of the parishes

MINI-OLYMPIC GAMES

In 1985, the International Olympic Committee approved the creation of the Games of the Small States of Europe (GSSE). The games are a six-day mini-Olympics held every other year for European nations with populations of less than 1 million inhabitants. The member nations are Andorra, Cyprus, Iceland, Liechtenstein, Luxembourg, Malta, Monaco, and San Marino. Ten sporting events, including basketball, swimming, volleyball, tennis, and judo, make up the games. Andorra hosted the most recent games, in 2005, when the Andorran swimmer Hocine Haciane dominated the swimming competition, winning five gold medals and one silver medal.

Andorra's Alex Antor training for his Men's Downhill event during the Winter Olympic Games in 2006.

now have ski clubs for different age groups. Soccer, shooting, and climbing clubs followed, and Andorra organized the Andorran Olympic Committee in 1971. On May 14, 1975, Andorra, with a population of 25,000, was accepted as a member of the world Olympic movement. Coincidentally on that same day China, with a population of almost 1 billion, was also accepted into the Olympic movement. Andorran athletes have participated in every international summer and winter Olympics since 1976. Andorra la Vella recently presented a proposal to the International Olympic Committee to host the XXI Olympic Winter Games, in 2010.

Ice racing is one of the most unusual sporting events in the world. Automobile drivers are normally instructed to drive cautiously on ice, but in ice racing the opposite is true. High-powered cars with talented drivers speed around professionally designed tracks, sliding into every curve and frequently crashing into the walls that surround the track. The Grandvalira Track at El Pas de la Casa is now the site of one of the major races in the French Andros Trophy Series. The track at Grandvalira is

slightly over half a mile (0.9 km) in length and is located at the highest elevation of any track in Europe, at 7,776 feet (2,370 m). Preparations for the race begin weeks in advance of the event, with regular spraying of water to build a thick, stable coating of ice.

The Pirena is held each December if the snow depth and quality permit. This 15-day sled dog race through the Pyrenees Mountains is a popular race on the European Sled Dog circuit and attracts some of the best dog teams from around the globe. It is the only sled dog race in the world where the course passes through three separate countries: Spain, Andorra, and France.

It seems as if every boy in Europe wants to grow up to be an international soccer star. However, this is not the case in Andorra, where rugby is a more popular sport than soccer. The Andorran National Rugby Team is nicknamed El Isards (The Isards), in recognition of the most popular animal in Andorra. Andorra fields a tough team that holds its own against teams from much larger countries. The team was listed in the top 50

Andorra's national rugby team is nicknamed The Isards, after the national animal of Andorra.

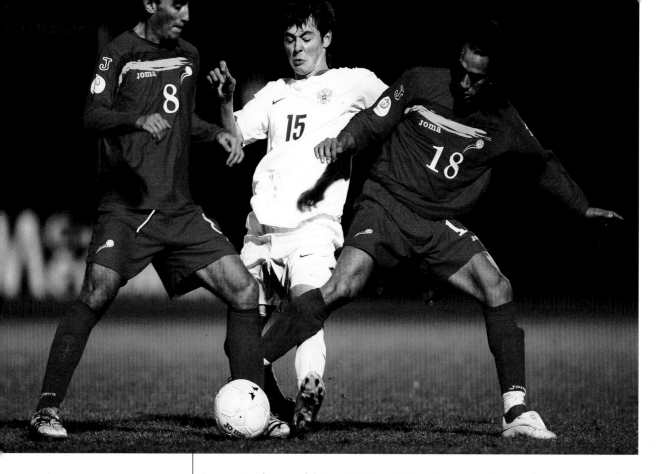

teams in the world in a 2007 ranking. Seventy-nine nations were ranked below the Isards, and during the 2007 World Cup play-offs, Andorra shocked Norway with a 76-3 defeat.

The National Soccer Team has not fared as well, winning only three games in its first 10 years of existence. Albert Celades, an Andorran citizen, is a world-class soccer player who has played for Real Zaragoza, Bordeaux, Real Madrid, Celta de Vigo, and Barcelona, some of the best professional soccer clubs in Europe. Unfortunately, he has chosen to play on the Spanish national team rather than Andorra's national team. The Andorran lack of interest in soccer was highlighted in a 2004 World Cup qualifying match with Macedonia, when fewer than 200 spectators attending.

ENTERTAINMENT

Per capita, more opportunities exist in Andorra for a variety of entertainment activities than in most countries in Europe. Andorrans participate in great numbers in the numerous religious and secular festivals held around the country. They attend classical music concerts, jazz festivals, theater productions, and opera competitions. They hold *festa del barri* (street parties), where grilled beef, chicken, lamb, sausage, cheese, and plenty of wine and beer are made available. During the ski season the nightclubs are jammed with young Andorrans and tourists dancing to the latest European and American music. Older Andorrans prefer spending a quiet night in a neighborhood restaurant, enjoying delicious Andorran cuisine with a glass of wine and music playing quietly in the background. For relaxation a day or evening at one of Andorra's outstanding thermal spas is a reward for a long week of work.

Many families like to spend quiet evenings at home, enjoying each other's company. Time is set aside to watch a little television, read, or play a game of chess, which remains popular in Andorra. Children enjoy modern technology by using computers, playing video games, chatting on their cell phones or the Internet, or listening to music on their iPods.

WEEKEND GETAWAYS

Sometimes Andorrans like to reverse the flow of tourist traffic into the country and depart for Spain and France for a weekend of leisure. Barcelona, one of Europe's most interesting cities, is a short three-hour drive away. The Costa Brava and stunning Mediterranean beaches are within a half day's drive. Leaving El Pas de la Casa, the medieval walled city of Carcassonne in France is only 80 miles (129 km) away. Tours of noted wineries, such as the Corbières vineyards, are accessible in a few hours. The French Riviera, with its beaches and the casinos of Nice and Monaco, provide attractive alternatives for spending leisure time within easy driving distance of home.

FESTIVALS

ANDORRA IS A NATION THAT always seems to be celebrating some special event or festival. It seems impossible to go through an entire week without the opportunity to participate in a music festival, religious holiday, theater production, exhibit, or some type of arts and crafts activity. Many of the celebrations are a combination of religious and secular activities. Some are sponsored by the national government, some by the parishes, and many by local villages and hamlets. Almost all include good food, good wine, traditional dances, music, and a special camaraderie among the people, regardless of whether they are citizens, foreign workers, or tourists.

RELIGIOUS FESTIVALS

The most widely celebrated religious holiday in Andorra occurs on September 8, a national holiday that honors the patron saint of Andorra, Our Lady of Meritxell. Thousands of pilgrims flock to the Sanctuary at Meritxell from all over the country, and even from France and Spain. After a solemn mass the faithful return to their homes for family dinners and to prepare for celebrations in all of the parishes, which feature concerts, exhibitions, fireworks, and dances.

The second most important religious celebration takes place on the last Sunday in May at the Sanctuary of the Virgin of Canòlich. The restored sanctuary contains an old wood carving of the Virgin Mary that was saved from the fire that destroyed the original building. The new sanctuary is located high on a hill above the Os River valley and has a panoramic view of some of the highest mountains in Andorra. Many of the pilgrims who come to attend the special mass remain after the service and picnic on the grounds of the church, consuming sausages, ham, chicken, lamb, or rabbit.

Opposite: **Andorrans of all ages participate in an open chess competition during the annual Village Festival in Andorra la Vella.**

The rest of the religious calendar includes several national holidays, such as Epiphany, the Assumption, All Saint's Day, the Immaculate Conception, Christmas, St. Steven's Day, Good Friday, Easter Monday, and Whitsun Monday. All Saint's Day, which falls on November 1, is celebrated not only in Andorra but in many countries around the world. The Catholic Church sets aside this day to honor all saints, known and unknown. Many Andorrans visit cemeteries on this date to place flowers on the graves of loved ones.

RELIGIOUS/SECULAR FESITVALS

Several religious holidays involve secular celebrations. On January 5, all of the parishes sponsor the Three Wise Men Processions. As the three men representing the magi pass through the town, they toss candy to excited children who in turn hand letters with requests for gifts to these visitors from afar.

Saint Anthony's Day, January 17, celebrates one of the most popular saints in the Catholic faith. During his time he was recognized as a great miracle worker, but today the faithful pray to him to help them find lost objects. On that day, all of the parishes hold events that center on the tasting of *escudella*, a traditional stew cooked in a cast-iron pot over a wood fire. The stew contains veal, chicken, salt pork, sausage, several types of vegetables, rice, and large flat noodles. It is frequently served with warm wine from a *porrò* (a typical Catalan drinking vessel with a thin spout). To consume the wine, people open their mouths wide and begin to drink the wine while extending their arms far from their bodies to produce a lengthy stream of wine from the *porrò* to their mouths. It is a skill that takes some practice and frequently leads to wine-colored stains on shirts and blouses.

Saint George's Day is celebrated on April 23 to honor a Roman soldier who protested against the torture of Christians and was killed because of his beliefs. The secular aspect of this celebration is the practice of exchanging special gifts between men and women. Men give their girlfriends or wives roses, while women give their boyfriends or husbands books. More roses and books are sold on this day than at any other time of the year. In addition, free admission to three popular museums offers people the opportunity to participate in an event that teaches about Andorran literature and includes a free book raffle.

UNESCO has declared Saint George's Day the International Day of the Book.

THE LEGEND OF THE PIPER OF ORDINO

Each August, Ordino holds its popular Bagpipe Festival. Pipers from all over Europe gather for the competition, which includes exhibitions, concerts, and parades. The event was initiated to celebrate the legend of the piper of Ordino.

According to the legend the people of Canillo hired one of the best bagpipe players in the country to perform at a festival for them. However, he did not arrive on schedule, causing great concern in Canillo, and then anger. When the piper arrived very late for his appointment, he told an interesting story. He had started out early for his trip to Canillo but had stopped to eat lunch. While eating, he was startled to discover a pack of wolves growling and hovering behind him. He ran for his life, with his bagpipe in tow. With the wolves chomping at his heels, he started to climb a tree to escape. However, the bagpipe got stuck in the branches of the tree, and when he jerked to free it, a horrifying sound came out of the bagpipe. The terrible sound frightened the wolves, and they fled in a panic. The piper climbed down from the tree and resumed his journey to Canillo. He played his bagpipe all the way to make sure the wolves did not return. When the people of Canillo heard his story, they forgave his late arrival, and the festivities began.

The Midsummer Night's Eve celebration, on June 23, marks the birth of John the Baptist and is referred to as St. John's Day. The date also marks the summer solstice and the beginning of a new season, an event pagan societies celebrated before the beginning of Christianity. Pagan legend warned individuals not to walk by themselves near Fontargent, Envalira, and Engolasters after dark. On the night of Saint John's Day witches are rumored to engage in all types of mischief, and the devil may grab solitary walkers and carry them off to unhappy endings.

SECULAR FESTIVALS

During the three days that precede the start of Lent, Carnival celebrations erupt in all of the parishes, with parades in almost every village and city. Hundreds of children march through the streets in brightly colored costumes and papier-mâché masks with distorted features. Some represent the devil, while others represent witches, pirates, soldiers, ferocious animals, and other images. Without a doubt, the best Carnival celebrations are in Encamp, where local actors perform street theater productions of the Dance of the Bear and the Judgment of the Smugglers. In the Dance of the Bear a naughty bear engages in all kinds of mischief, to the crowd's delight, but goes too far when he tries to woo a local maiden. For this act he must be punished and dies at the hands of the brave local hunters, who defend the maiden's virtue. The Judgment of the Smugglers pokes fun at the time-honored tradition of smuggling in Andorra and keeps the audience laughing.

During three successive weeks in July the Plaça Sant Roc in Sant Julià de Lòria bursts to life with its highly acclaimed Summer Musical Evening's program. Tuesday night is music night, each one concentrating on a genre, including flamenco, eastern music, and rumba. On Wednesday nights spectators are treated to dancing exhibitions, including Cuban rhythms, tap dance, and Argentine folk dances. On Thursday nights acrobats, circus performers, and magicians frequently perform.

PARISH FESTIVALS

In the months of July, August, and September each parish has its own public holiday. These events are extremely popular and draw large crowds. Parades, traditional folk dances, music, and an abundance of good food highlight each of the festivals.

Many of the parades include giant figures, reaching close to 15 feet (4.45 m) in height that represent important mythical or historical characters from Andorra's past. Workers construct the figures on wooden racks, and stout men carry the structures on their shoulders while dancing and swirling

Decorations of colorful flags are put up during the parish festival of Andorra la Vella, held on the first Saturday of August. The festival lasts for three days.

along the parade route. One of the favorites is Andorra's White Lady. She always has a beautiful papier-mâché face and a white silk gown. The White Lady represents a lovely young woman who escaped her evil stepmother's plot to have her murdered, then met and fell in love with a handsome young prince, whom she married and lived with happily ever after.

TRADITIONAL DANCES

During the festivities two popular dances may be performed. The *marratxa* features two men wearing top hats decorated with long, flowing multicolored ribbons. Each of the men dances with three beautiful ladies, swirling through the streets of town. It has never been substantiated, but many Andorrans believe the two men represent the two co-princes and that the six female dancers represent the six original parishes of Andorra.

The *sardana* is a popular folk dance that is performed at almost all festivals. It is an expression of unity among the people of Catalan culture. The dance begins when a group of dancers joins hands and forms a circle. As the music starts, the dancers raise and lower their hands while moving clockwise and then counterclockwise in small but precise steps. Children learn the movements of the dance early in their lives and continue to participate in the *sardana* as senior citizens.

The music for the dance is provided by a special band that always includes two trumpets, a trombone, two *flügelhorns*, a bass, a flute, a small drum, two oboe-type instruments, and two tenores (English horns). The music and dancing energizes the crowd and creates an immense sense of cultural pride.

Although many people no longer wear traditional costumes for the dance, some of the professional groups do. The traditional costume for women features a full, long, flowered skirt over a white petticoat. It also includes a black blouse with elbow-length sleeves, white stockings, and black open-toe sandals. A crimson shawl is frequently draped over the shoulders and tied loosely in the front.

The traditional costume for men is a white long-sleeved shirt, open at the neck and covered with a black vest with brass buttons. The men's costume also includes black knee-length pants, with high stockings and black shoes. To add a splash of color, the men wear a crimson sash tied at the waist and a red hat with black trim called a *barretina*.

CALENDAR OF PUBLIC HOLIDAYS

* January 1	New Year's Day
– January 6	Epiphany
* March 14	Constitution Day
– May 1	Labor Day
– August 15	The Assumption
* September 8	National Holiday, Our Lady of Meritxell
– November 1	All Saint's Day
– December 8	The Immaculate Conception
* December 25	Christmas
– December 26	St. Stephen's Day

Movable Holidays
– February-March	Carnival Monday
– March-April	Good Friday
– March-April	Easter Monday
– May-June	Whitsun Monday

* Holidays with compulsory closing of all businesses.
- Holidays with compulsory closing for the building trades, industries in general, offices, banks, hairdressers, transport and delivery of goods, and any services not directly related to tourism.

FOOD

THE DIET AND POPULAR DISHES of Andorra are a reflection of the geographic conditions that limited the food items available to be produced. For most of the country's history it was isolated, and the significant importation of food products from outside areas did not exist. As a rural mountain society, meals consisted primarily of meat, home-grown garden vegetables and fruits, bread (especially dark rye bread made from locally grown rye), fish, and wild game. Those traditional foods still dominate the diets of today's Andorrans.

A PASTORAL SETTING

Livestock production has always characterized the agricultural sector of the Andorran economy. Sheep were the principal livestock raised,

Left: **Cattle are raised under controlled conditions in Andorra.**

Opposite: **Due to their geographical position, the Andorran diet was limited to what they could produce on their own, such as garden vegetables and bread.**

but almost all families also had a few beef and dairy cattle, some pigs, goats, chickens, and a few domesticated rabbits. The main techniques for cooking meat products today are largely the same as they were in the past. The most popular cooking technique is *carn a la brasa*, where slabs of meat are cooked on either indoor or outdoor grills using natural wood or charcoal. Many traditional restaurants have indoor, wood-burning grills, where the customer can see the grill while enjoying the aroma of the meat as it cooks. Roasted meat, especially lamb, is popular, and casserole dishes simmered slowly over a low fire are also favorites. Fried foods are not common, which may help explain the extended life span of Andorrans and their below-average incidence of heart problems and high blood pressure.

LAMB

Lamb remains one of the favored meats in Andorra. While most families either grill or roast the lamb in their homes, their favorite preparation method is to take a slab of lamb to the mountains on a hiking and camping trip, where they can prepare the meat in the traditional mountain style. A grill is set up over a bed of hot coals produced from the branches of the rhododendron shrub. The smoke from the rhododendron produces a light, smoky flavor that does not overwhelm the taste buds. A piece of natural slate rubbed with virgin olive oil is slowly heated over the coals until it is ready for cooking. The lamb is gently massaged with a mixture of olive oil, garlic, rosemary, and a little salt and is placed on the slate to cook slowly. Meanwhile, unpeeled potatoes wrapped in foil are placed in the ashes, near the edge of the fire. Fresh dandelion greens are tossed with hot bacon just as the lamb and potatoes are fully cooked.

Having a glass of wine with this simple Andorran-style mountain meal tops off a unique culinary experience.

OTHER MEATS AND ANIMAL PRODUCTS

Pork is also a very popular meat. Andorrans like to claim that they eat everything on the pig but its squeal. A variety of sausages are made, including blood sausage and head sausage. Some of the most delicious sausages are *butifarra*, *llonganissa*, and *bringuera*. The sausages are cooked on the grill most frequently but also end up in several types of soups and stews. One recipe for *escudella* calls for two pig ears. Ham is primarily eaten for breakfast, and a favorite choice is a slab of ham simmered in a skillet and served with honey.

Veal dishes are especially popular in Andorra, as are grilled steaks. Milk and cheese are consumed daily in Andorran homes and, historically, the favorite local cheese was *formatge de tupí*. This cheese is made from goat's milk that is fermented in a ceramic earthenware pot with garlic and brandy.

Rabbit can be found on the majority of restaurant menus and is listed by its Catalan name, *cunill*. The two most popular ways to eat rabbit are grilled and served with *allioli*, a Catalan type of mayonnaise, or stewed with an assortment of vegetables. Many rural residents build hutches for rabbits, and one of the children's chores is to care for the rabbits on a daily basis. Families consume the majority of the rabbits they raise, but surplus rabbit meat is also sold fresh in local stores. Restaurants will sometimes contract with farmers to obtain a regular supply of rabbit meat.

SEAFOOD

Fresh trout caught from clear mountain lakes and streams are the favorite fish of Andorra. Trout is frequently found on restaurant menus, and grilled trout is almost always a part of family hiking and camping experiences.

Trout is found frequently on restaurant menus in Andorra.

Since the opening of road connections to both Spain (1913) and France (1935), a variety of seafood has become available to Andorran consumers. Fresh seafood from both the Atlantic Ocean and the Mediterranean Sea arrives daily in refrigerated trucks. Fresh North Atlantic cod is rapidly growing in popularity, partly because of the influence of Portuguese nationals living in Andorra on work permits. It was also imported in the past, preserved in salt, so that it could easily reach the mountains without spoiling. Squid and octopus cooked in butter and garlic sauce are favorites of tourists.

WILD GAME

Although most Andorrans now live in urban areas, they love to hunt in the mountains. The isard is the most popular wild game, but hunters also try to bag wild pigs, hare, and squirrels. The isard is frequently simmered in a wine sauce flavored with chocolate; this dish is called *civet d'isard*. *Llebre* is hare simmered in its own blood with a variety of vegetables.

VEGETABLES AND FRUIT

Today most vegetables and fruit are purchased in modern supermarkets, but in the past they were grown on plots of land near the family home. Potatoes, cabbage, carrots, turnips, onions, tomatoes, and garlic were all common garden plants. One traditional dish in Andorra is *trinxat*, which is prepared by boiling a head of cabbage and several potatoes until they are well cooked and tender. The water is drained from the cabbage and potatoes, and they are diced into small pieces and fried slowly with garlic and bacon until the bacon is crisp. *Trinxat* is frequently served with salted herring and pimentos. Stews such as *escudella* contain an

Fast-food
restaurants in
Andorra include
McDonalds,
Burger King,
Pizza Hut,
Kentucky Fried
Chicken, and
Quik, a French
chain.

Foie gras is a delicious
appetizer.

assortment of fresh vegetables. Most fresh fruit is now imported from
Spain and France, where their Mediterranean climates encourage fruit
and nut production. Oranges, lemons, plums, peaches, and apples are
all major imports.

SPECIALTY FOODS

Perhaps the most common food eaten in Andorra is an appetizer called
pa amb tomàquet. It is a slice of toasted bread smeared with a crushed
paste of garlic and tomato, drizzled with olive oil and sprinkled with
salt. *Truita de carreroles* are similar to omelets and sometimes are served
on a flaky piece of pastry. *Allioli* is a Catalan type of mayonnaise made
from garlic cloves, eggs, a little lemon juice, and salt, whipped to a

creamy texture with olive oil. It is spread on bread, baked on cod, and used as a dip for sausages and other meats.

One of the main reasons Andorrans enjoy hiking and camping in the mountains is the opportunity those experiences offer to hunt for wild herbs, celery, berries, and mushrooms. In fact, Andorrans have been long referred to as mycophilics, or mushroom lovers. While wild mushrooms can be found during most months of the year, they are especially abundant from September through November. During these months several restaurants that serve traditional Andorran foods serve three-course meals that consist of nothing but delicious dishes cooked with mushrooms.

FRENCH INFLUENCES

Although the impact of Catalan cooking has left the biggest imprint on Andorran cuisine, French cuisine also played an important role. Small, family-owned French restaurants can be found in many cities and villages, and French chefs dominate many of the large hotel kitchens. The French are unchallenged experts at creating sauces from cream and wine that dramatically enhance the flavor of meats and excite the taste buds. Duck and veal are their specialties, and they are masters of preparation and presentation. Snails and foie gras (duck or goose liver) make delicious appetizers. Few people understand the complex relationship between wine and food better than the French, and their restaurants are stocked with the best wine selections. Completing a meal with a delicate, flaky French pastry topped with a raspberry or strawberry sauce completes a voyage to culinary heaven.

It is an Andorran tradition to make cannelloni on Saint Stephen's Day from meat leftovers from Christmas celebrations.

FOOD FESTIVALS

In a nation whose inhabitants enjoy food as much as the Andorrans, it is not surprising that there are several festivals whose central theme is food. None of these celebrations is as popular as the festival of the *escudella* on Saint Anthony's Day in all of the parishes and Saint Sebastian's Day in Sant Julià de Lòria. The people's favorite by far is held on the Plaça de la Germandat in Sant Julià de Lòria. Huge pots of steaming *escudella*, a stew that contains at least five different types of meat, six or seven vegetables, rice, and noodles, are scattered around the square. Visitors form lines for blocks, waiting for their free meal of *escudella*, bread, and wine. In February the French influence is apparent in a 15-day truffle celebration sponsored by La Fogaina dels Pirineus. During these winter days seven restaurants create elegant Andorran cuisine with special dishes made with truffles. The Sardine and Soup-Tasting Festival occurs in Ordino during the Carnival season. Free roasted chestnut festivals abound in all of the parishes on All Saint's Day. Salt Cod Day is an event that celebrates different ways to cook and serve cod. The nation celebrates, in September, the traditional dishes of Andorra with food and wine sampling at the Gastronomic Fair of Andorra.

BEVERAGES

Most parents drink coffee with breakfast, while the children consume milk or fruit juice. During the day workers take a break and have a cup of coffee, espresso, or latte if a specialty shop is close to work. Wine is frequently served with the family meal in the evenings, and older children are permitted to have a glass of wine with their parents. Beer is a popular beverage for picnics, while grilling meat, and during parish festivals. A cup of hot chocolate or a glass of heated wine or moscatel tops off a vigorous day of skiing.

MEALTIME

Breakfast is frequently eaten on the run. Children are off to school, and in many homes both parents need to leave early for work. Choices may include a bowl of cereal, an egg with a selection of cold cuts (salami, prosciutto, ham), or some cheese. A basket of fresh fruit is almost always within reach and, for those in a hurry, a fresh pastry may be all that time permits.

A hearty snack of bread, sausage, grilled artichoke, fries, and a glass of beer.

Schoolchildren almost always eat their midday meals in school cafeterias or bring their own lunch. Adults will slip out of work for lunch to a nearby deli or neighborhood restaurant. A slice of pizza, a variety of pastries stuffed with meat or cheese, and sandwiches are common choices. Workers generally eat close to their place of employment. They do not want to take their cars out of the parking garages and get stuck in traffic, which can substantially delay their return to work.

Normally the evening meal is reserved for family time. It is served late by American standards (8:00 to 9:00 P.M.) and is usually consumed at a leisurely pace. Traditional Andorran food is favored, with large servings of meat, vegetables, and a rich dessert.

PA AMB TOMÀQUET (TOASTED BREAD WITH OLIVE OIL, TOMATO, GARLIC, AND HERBS)

Andorran families love to prepare this delicious appetizer when they are camping in the mountains. However, it is also popular at home and can be grilled outdoors or toasted indoors in an oven. Grilling the bread over a charcoal fire will enhance the flavor. This recipe serves six.

6 slices country bread, cut 1 inch thick
$\frac{1}{3}$ cup extra-virgin olive oil
2 garlic cloves, peeled and halved
1 large ripe tomato, halved
2 tablespoons *herbes de Provence*

Have an adult light the charcoal fire in a grill. Brush both sides of the bread slices with the olive oil. Grill the bread over a moderately hot fire until lightly charred, about 1 minute for each side. Rub the hot toasts with the garlic halves, then the ripe tomato halves. Make sure some of the tomato pulp soaks into the bread. Sprinkle the toasts with the *herbes de Provence*, and serve while hot.

ANDORRAN/CATALAN SPINACH SALAD

Many Andorrans like to begin their meal with this popular salad. This recipe serves four.

2 bunches fresh spinach
2 tablespoons extra-virgin olive oil
1 garlic clove, peeled and sliced
$1/3$ cup raisins
$1/3$ cup pine nuts (or 1/3 cup almonds)

Wash the spinach thoroughly, then chop and blanch it. To blanch the spinach, dip it in boiling water for a few seconds, remove, and place in ice water. Simmer the olive oil and garlic in a pan until the garlic turns golden, and then add the raisins and nuts, cooking until the raisins are plump. Drain the spinach, and place it in a bowl. Pour the oil, raisin, garlic, and nut mixture over the spinach, and serve.

A   **B**   **C**   **D**

1

F R A N C E

P y r e n e e s

Pic de Tristaina
(9435ft / 2876m)

Pic de la Font Blanca
(9424ft / 2903m)

Tristaina River

● El Serrat

Pic de la Serrera
(9553ft / 2912m)

2

Angonella River

North Valira River

Pic de l'Estanyó
(9563ft / 2915m) ▲

▲ Pic de Comapedrosa
(9652ft / 2942m)

● Llorts

Montaup River

Riu River

Coma River

Incles River

Pic de la Cabaneta
(9274ft / 2827m)

● Arinsal

● La Cortinada

Ransol ●

● Soldeu

● Erts

● Somàs

Canillo ●

East Valira River

3

Pal ●

Pal River

Arinsal River

● Ordino

A N D O R R A

● La Massana

Encamp ●

Cortals River

Alt del Griu
(9429ft / 2874m) ▲

El Pas de ●
la Casa

Monyaner River

Ensagents River

Pic d'Envalira
(9274ft / 2827m) ▲

● Engordany

East Valira River

ANDORRA LA VELLA ●

● Les Escaldes

Pic de Ribus
(9274ft / 2827m) ▲

Madriu River

■ Madriu-Perafita-
Claror Valley

■ Pont de la
Margineda

Aixovall ●

Os River

Tossa Plana de Lles
(9566ft / 2916m) ▲

4

Sant Julià ●
de Lòria

Valira River

5

S P A I N

N

●	Capital city
●	Major town
▲	Mountain peak
■	Ancient site

Feet		Meters
16,500		5,000
9,900		3,000
6,600		2,000
3,300		1,000
1,650		500
660		200
0		0

MAP OF ANDORRA

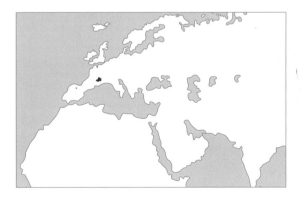

ECONOMIC ANDORRA

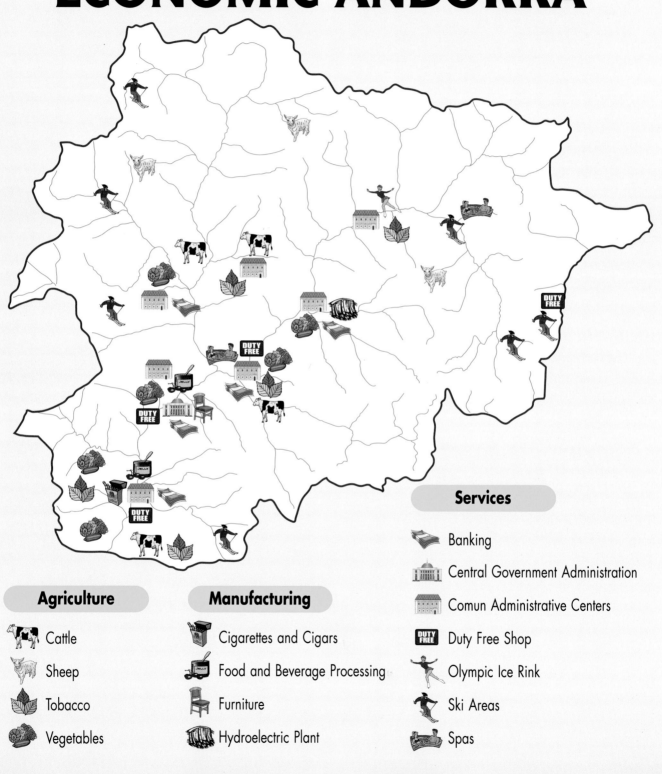

Agriculture
- Cattle
- Sheep
- Tobacco
- Vegetables

Manufacturing
- Cigarettes and Cigars
- Food and Beverage Processing
- Furniture
- Hydroelectric Plant

Services
- Banking
- Central Government Administration
- Comun Administrative Centers
- Duty Free Shop
- Olympic Ice Rink
- Ski Areas
- Spas

ABOUT THE ECONOMY

GDP
US$ 2.77 billion (2005)

PER CAPITA GDP
US$ 38,800 (2005)

GDP SECTORS
Agriculture 0.3 percent; construction 15.3 percent; manufacturing 4.3 percent; services (commerce, hotels, restaurants, banking, government services, etc.) 80.1 percent (2005)

LAND AREA
175 square miles (468 sq km)

FORESTED LANDS
38.23 percent (2005)

UNEMPLOYMENT RATE
Less than 1 percent (2005)

CURRENCY
Andorra has no official currency. Andorra uses the euro for its currency.
USD 1 = EUR 0.68 (2007)

AGRICULTURAL PRODUCTS
Tobacco, sheep, cattle, hay, vegetables

INDUSTRIES
Cigarettes and cigars, furniture, food and beverage processing, publishing and graphic arts, electricity production and distribution

MAJOR EXPORTS
Machines and electrical appliances, motor vehicles, tractors, motorbikes, bicycles, sugars and candy

MAJOR IMPORTS
Machines and electrical appliances, motor vehicles, tractors, motorbikes, bicycles, perfumes and toiletry products

MAJOR TRADING PARTNERS
Spain, France, Germany

PORTS, HARBORS, AIRPORTS, TRAIN STATIONS
None

INFLATION RATE
3.2 percent (2005)

POVERTY RATE
0 percent (2005)

LEADING FOREIGN INVESTORS
European Union (EU)

CULTURAL ANDORRA

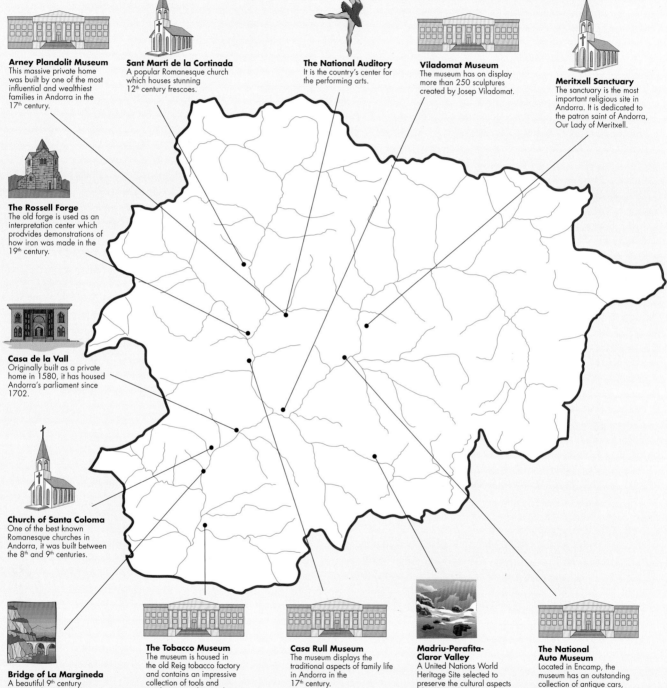

Arney Plandolit Museum
This massive private home was built by one of the most influential and wealthiest families in Andorra in the 17th century.

Sant Martí de la Cortinada
A popular Romanesque church which houses stunning 12th century frescoes.

The National Auditory
It is the country's center for the performing arts.

Viladomat Museum
The museum has on display more than 250 sculptures created by Josep Viladomat.

Meritxell Sanctuary
The sanctuary is the most important religious site in Andorra. It is dedicated to the patron saint of Andorra, Our Lady of Meritxell.

The Rossell Forge
The old forge is used as an interpretation center which prodvides demonstrations of how iron was made in the 19th century.

Casa de la Vall
Originally built as a private home in 1580, it has housed Andorra's parliament since 1702.

Church of Santa Coloma
One of the best known Romanesque churches in Andorra, it was built between the 8th and 9th centuries.

Bridge of La Margineda
A beautiful 9th century Roman-style stone bridge which crosses the Valira River.

The Tobacco Museum
The museum is housed in the old Reig tobacco factory and contains an impressive collection of tools and machinery used in producing cigarettes and cigars.

Casa Rull Museum
The museum displays the traditional aspects of family life in Andorra in the 17th century.

Madriu-Perafita-Claror Valley
A United Nations World Heritage Site selected to preserve the cultural aspects of traditional mountain life.

The National Auto Museum
Located in Encamp, the museum has an outstanding collection of antique cars, motorcycles, and bicycles.

ABOUT THE CULTURE

OFFICIAL NAME
Principality of Andorra

CAPITAL
Andorra la Vella

OTHER MAJOR CITIES
Escaldes-Engordany, Encamp, Sant Julià de Lòria, La Massana

NATIONAL FLAG
The flag is divided into three equal vertical stripes, with blue on the hoist side, yellow in the center, and red on the outer side. The Andorran coat of arms is centered in the yellow stripe.

NATIONAL ANTHEM
"El Gran Carlemany" ("The Great Charlemagne") was adopted on September 8, 1914, with the lyrics written by Joan Benlloch i Vivò, bishop of Urgell and coprince of Andorra from 1906 to 1919.

OFFICIAL LANGUAGE
Catalan

POPULATION
78,549 (2005)

POPULATION DENSITY
449 per square mile (168 per sq km)

ETHNIC GROUPS
Andorrans 35.97 percent; Spanish 35.74 percent; Portuguese 14.38 percent; French 6.46 percent; British 1.3 percent; other 6.1 percent

LIFE EXPECTANCY
Female 86.62 years; Male 80.62 years

RELIGIONS
Roman Catholic 90 percent; minority religions Anglicans, Jehovah's Witness, Church of Jesus Christ of Latter-day Saints (Mormons), Muslims, Jews, and a few Hindus and Buddhists

EDUCATION
Free and compulsory to age 16

LITERACY RATE
100 percent

CO-PRINCES OF ANDORRA
Joan Enric Vives i Sicilía, bishop of Urgell
Nicolas Sarkozy, president of France

NATIONAL HOLIDAY
Our Lady of Meritxell (September 8)

LEADERS IN THE ARTS
Gerard Claret (violin soloist and conductor of the National Chamber Orchestra of Andorra), Lluís Claret (cellist), Albert Salvadó (writer)

TIME LINE

IN ANDORRA	IN THE WORLD

2000 B.C.
Human skeletal remains left near La Margineda.

219–218 B.C.
Greek historian Polybius notes the presence of the Andosinos in eastern Pyrenees.

323 B.C.
Alexander the Great's empire stretches from Greece to India.

A.D. 711–732
Muslim Moors move through the valleys of Andorra from Spain to France.

732
Charles Martel defeats the Moors at the Battle of Poitiers.

839
Act of Consecration and Assignment of the Cathedral of Seu d'Urgell acknowledges the existence of Andorra.

843
Valleys of Andorra ceded to Sunifred I, count of Urgell.

1000
The Chinese perfect gunpowder and begin to use it in warfare.

1100
Rise of the Incan Civilization in Peru.

1133
Authority over Andorra passes to the bishops of Urgell.

1206–1368
Genghis Khan unifies the Mongols and starts conquest of the world. At its height, the Mongol Empire under Kublai Khan stretches from China to Persia and parts of Europe and Russia.

1278
First *pareatge* signed, creating the modern Principality of Andorra.

1288
Second *pareatge* signed, confirming the bishop of Urgell and the count of Foix as coprinces of Andorra.

1419
Official creation of the Council of the Land.

1558–1603
Reign of Elizabeth I of England

1748
Publication of the Manual Digest.

1776
U.S. Declaration of Independence

IN ANDORRA	IN THE WORLD
	1789–99 The French Revolution
1806 Napoleon I reestablishes the French co-prince.	
	1861 The U.S. Civil War begins.
1866 The New Reform is ratified.	
1913 The first road linking Andorra to the outside world, to Spain, is completed.	**1869** The Suez Canal is opened.
	1914 World War I begins.
1933 Baron Boris de Skossyreff proclaims himself King Boris I of Andorra and is arrested.	**1939** World War II begins.
	1941 Japan attacks Pearl Harbor.
	1945 The United States drops atomic bombs on Hiroshima and Nagasaki.
1952 Andorra signs its first international agreement.	**1949** The North Atlantic Treaty Organization (NATO) is formed.
1970 Women obtain the right to vote.	**1966–69** The Chinese Cultural Revolution.
1981 Executive Council and the office of Head of Government are established.	**1986** Nuclear power disaster at Chernobyl in Ukraine
1993 Andorran citizens ratify the Constitution of the Principality of Andorra; Andorra joins the United Nations.	**1991** Breakup of the Soviet Union.
1994 Marc Forné Molné is elected head of government.	**1997** Hong Kong is returned to China.
	2001 Terrorists crash planes in New York, Washington D.C., and Pennsylvania.
2005 Albert Pintat Santolària is elected head of government.	**2003** War in Iraq begins.

GLOSSARY

bander
A game warden in Andorra who is responsible for protecting the country's natural environment, including plants and animals.

camaraderie
A spirit of warm, friendly feelings among companions.

comuns
The local administrative governments of the seven parishes of Andorra

culinary
Relating to the art of cooking or the creation of food.

edifice
A building.

frescoes
Wall paintings found on the walls of many Romanesque churches in Andorra.

gastronomic
Relating to the art or science of good eating.

ingot
A mass of metal cast under extreme heat into a bar or other convenient shape.

metamorphic
A type of rock that has changed in texture, structure, and mineral makeup under pressure and heat. Slate is a metamorphic rock that began as shale.

moscatel
A rich, sweet wine made from the muscat variety of grape.

patriarchal
A society that is dominated by men.

prosciutto
A spicy cured ham served as thin, delicate slices.

promontory
A high piece of land that allows a view of the area below.

radiocarbon dating
A technique scientists use to measure the age of dead plant and animal material.

raucous
Behavior that is rough-sounding, loud, and rowdy.

sovereign
One who is not controlled by others, but rather is independent.

truffle
A fleshy, edible type of fungi that grows underground and is regarded as a delicacy in many parts of the world.

unicameral
Having a single legislative chamber of representatives.

FURTHER INFORMATION

BOOKS

Davis, Charles. *Walk! Andorra*. Northampton: Discover Walking Guides, Ltd., 2005.

Eccardt, Thomas. *Secrets of the Seven Smallest States of Europe*. New York: Hippocrene Books, Inc., 2005.

Leckey, Colin. *Dots on the Map*. Guildford: Grosvenor House Publishing Ltd., 2006.

Ring, Trudy. *International Dictionary of Historic Places: Southern Europe*. New York: Routledge, 1996.

Robertson, Alf, and Jane Meadowcraft. *The Mountains of Andorra: Walks, Scrambles, Via Ferratas, Treks*. Milnthorpe: Cicerone Press, 2005.

WEB SITES

A Brief Catalan Tutorial. www.catalunya-lliure.com/curs/pronounce.html

Catalan Pronunciation. www.orbilat.com/Languages/Catalan/Grammar/Catalan-Pronunciation.html

CIA World Factbook. https://www.cia.gov/library/publications/the-world-factbook/geos/an.html

Govern d'Andorra Recipies. www.andorra.ad/ang/gaudeix_andorra/gastronomia/plats_tipics.asp

The Andorran Institutions. www.andorra.be/en/2.4.htm

The Constitution of the Principality of Andorra. www.andorramania.com/constit_gb.htm

The Map Archive. www.maparchive.org/details.php?image_id=47

The Museums of Andorra. www.hola-andorra.com/arinsal/english/museumsgb.html

U.S. Department of State Background Note: Andorra. www.state.gov/r/palei/bgn/3164.htm

MUSIC

Bach: 6 Cello Suites BWV 1007–1012. Lluís Claret. Verso, 2006.

Concert. The National Choir of Young Singers of Andorra. Capital Sound Studios, 2005.

Eurovision Song Contest: Helsinki 2007. Various Artists. EMI International, 2007.

Music for String Orchestra. Andorra National Chamber Orchestra. Nimbus, 2003.

MAP

Kuehn, Eva. *International Travel Maps: Andorra*. Vancouver: ITMB Publishing, 2004.

BIBLIOGRAPHY

Chamber of Commerce, Industry, and Services. Economic Report 2005. Andorra la Vella, Andorra, 2006.
_____. Andorra 2006. Andorra la Vella, Andorra, 2007.

Duursma, Jorri. *Fragmentation and the International Relations of Micro-States.* Cambridge: Cambridge University Press, 1996.

Estaban, Pere, Philip D. Jones, Javier Martin-Vide, and Montse Mases. "Atmospheric Circulation Patterns Related to Heavy Snowfall Days in Andorra, Pyrenees." International Journal of Climatology, 25 (February 11, 2005) 319–29.

Government of Andorra, Ministry of Foreign Affairs. Cooperation Andorra. Andorra la Vella, Andorra, 2007.

_____. Ministry of Tourism. Andorra: Cultural Itineraries. Andorra la Vella, Andorra, 2004.

_____. Secretary of State for the Agency Andorra 2020. Andorra 2020 Program. Andorra la Vella, Andorra, 2007.

Peattie, Roderick. "Andorra; A Study in Mountain Geography." Geographical Review, 19 (April, 1929) 218-33.

Standard and Poors Credit Research Report. Andorra. New York, NY: McGraw-Hill Companies, 2006.

Taylor, Bayard. *The Republic of the Pyrenees: Andorra 1867.* Andorra la Vella, Andorra: Government of Andorra, 2002.

INDEX